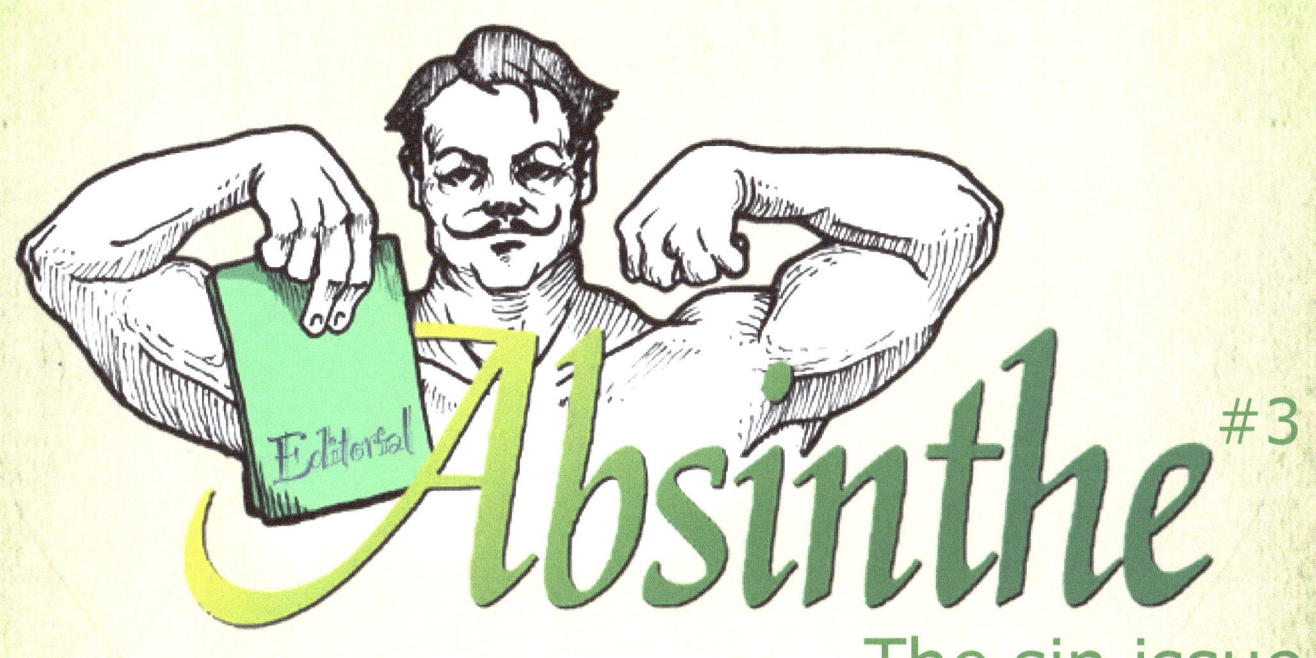

Editorial

Absinthe #3

The sin issue

May 2011

Colaborators:

Cover: Alexey Malina

Artist:
Mateusz Kolek
Poland

URL:
http://mateuszkolek.com

I have a question that's bothering me
its all about little boys
Why are they scruffy and so unkind
and why do they make all that noise
I normally wouldn't bother so much
but the answer I must find you see
Because I have three of the most horrible kind
living in this house with me
Wait a minute perhaps that's unkind,
Its obvious how silly of me
I have made the mistake of comparing them with girls
who naturally are all perfect like me.

Written by: John Mullan (Written with girls in mind)

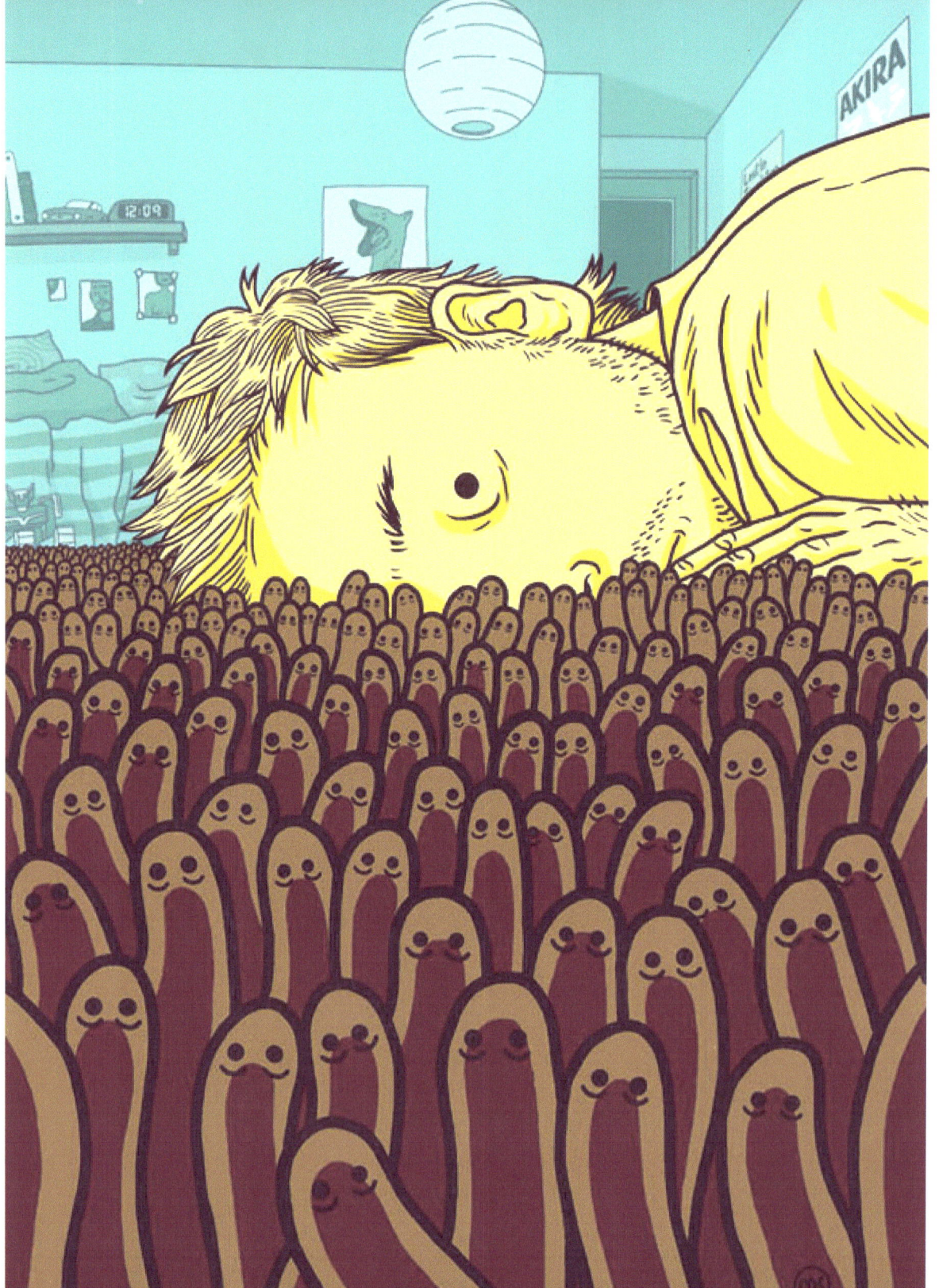

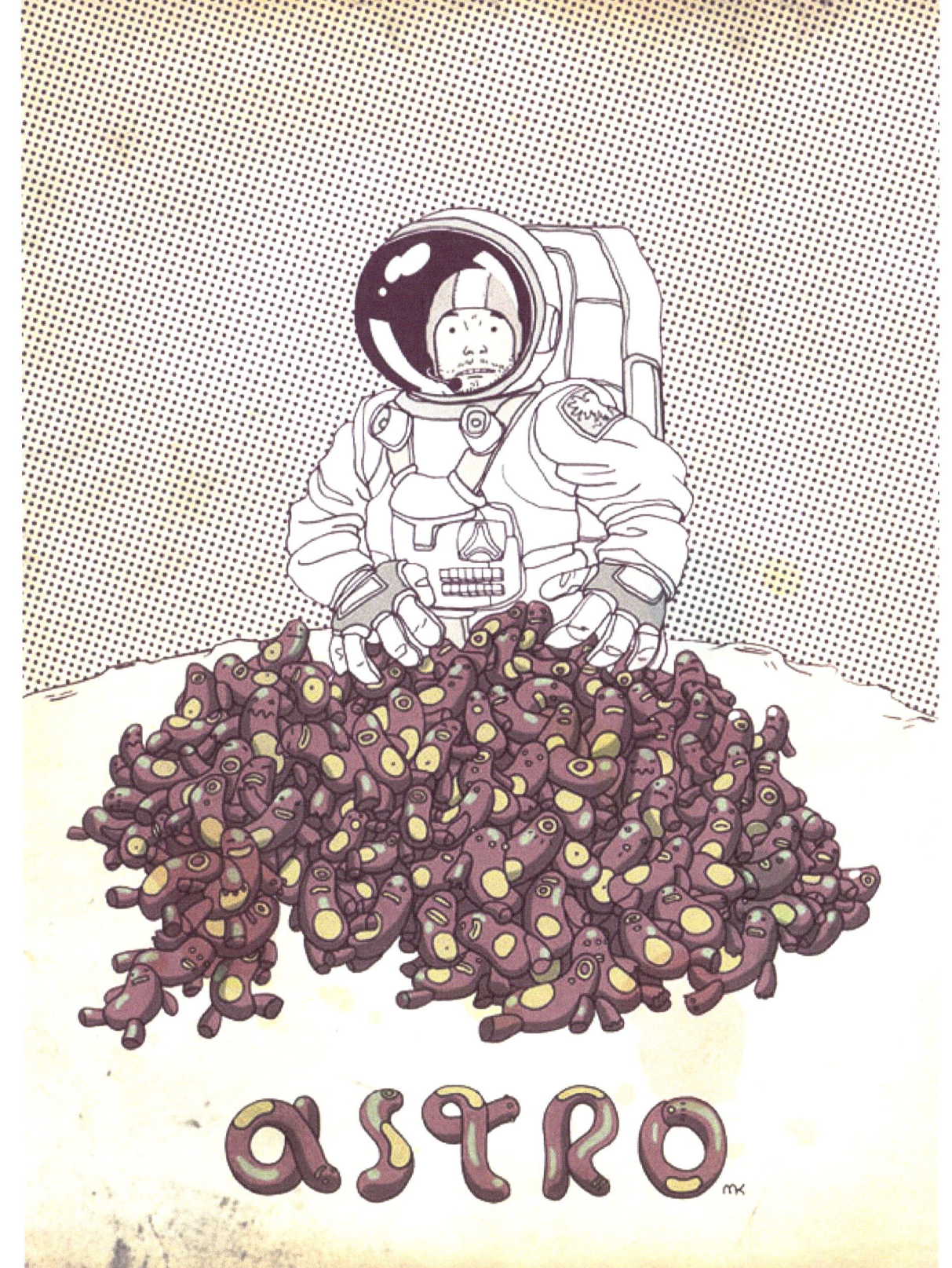

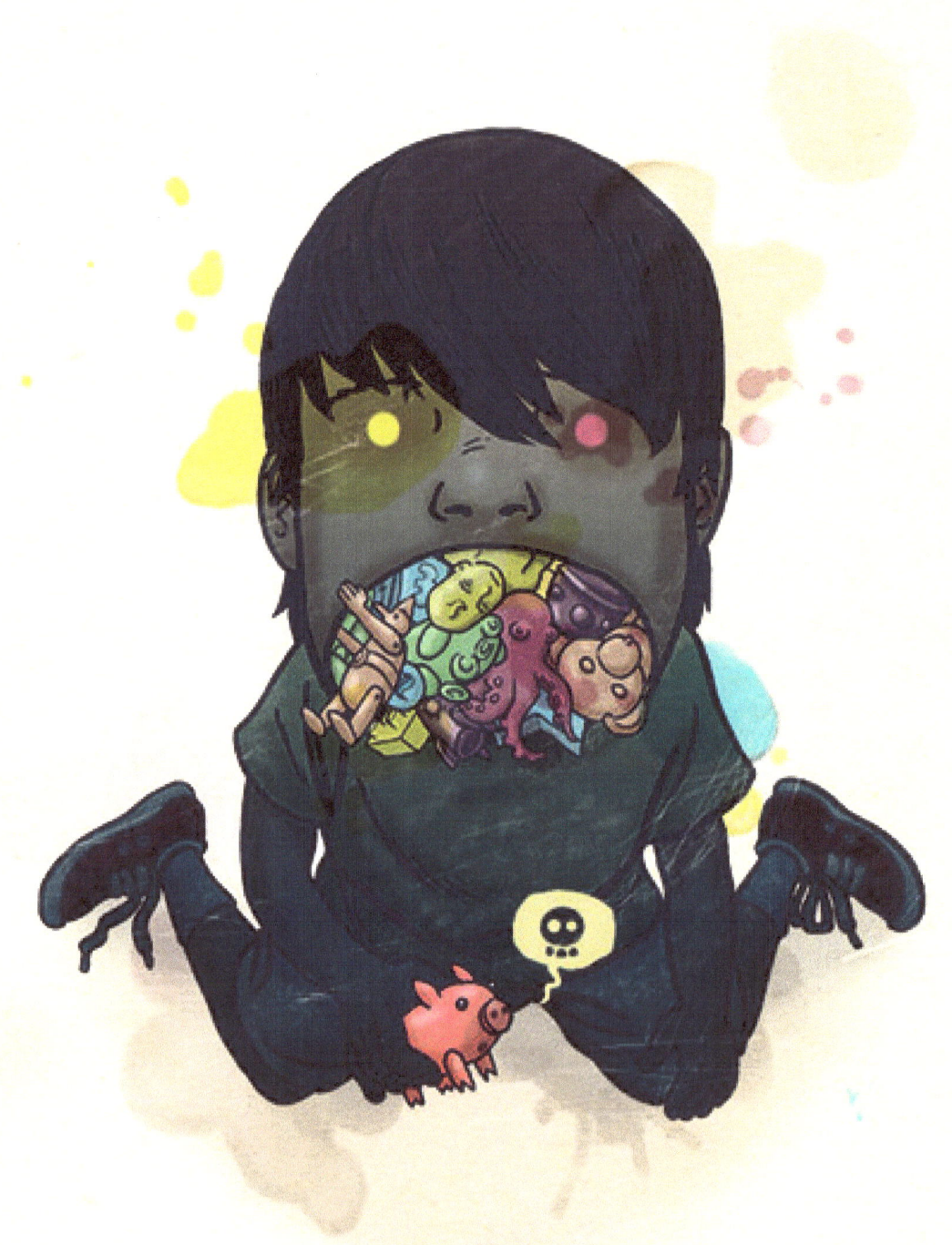
Toyea

Artist:

Isabel Nadal
Spain

URL:
http://isabelnadal.es

Be wary of Greed it's a cunning creature
that sneaks up behind your back
It starts with „wouldn't it be nice to have"
and
ends with „I must have that"
At first quite small it soon grows tall it has
an enormous appetite
An equal share wouldn't do at all, but that
just can't be right
So don't stand still worrying too much that
its old instead of new
Because as you stand dreaming about
what you want next
Greed will creep up on you.

Written by: John Mullan

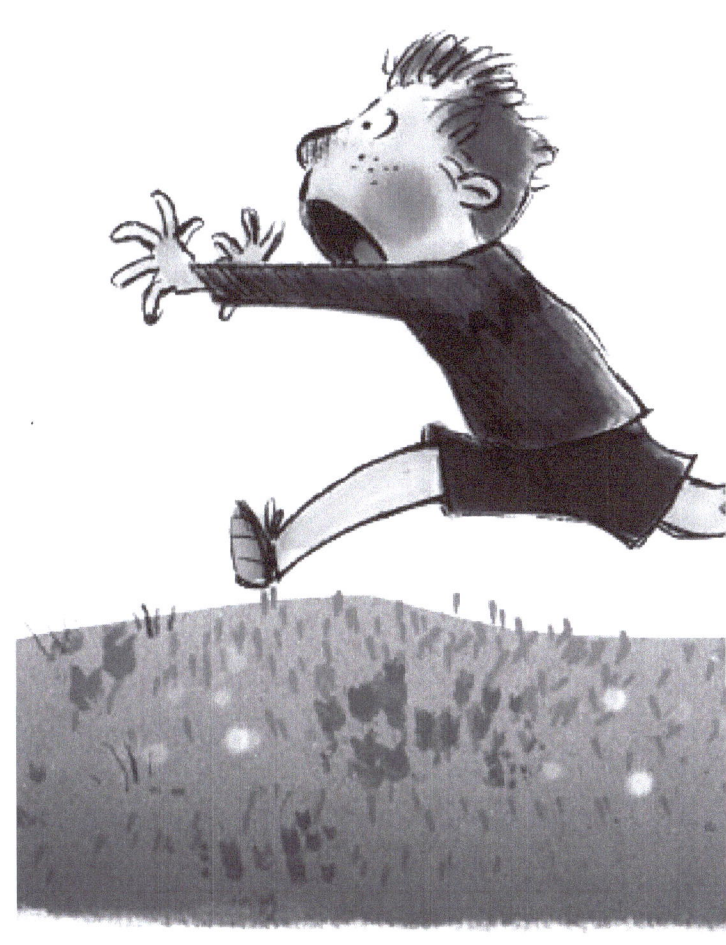

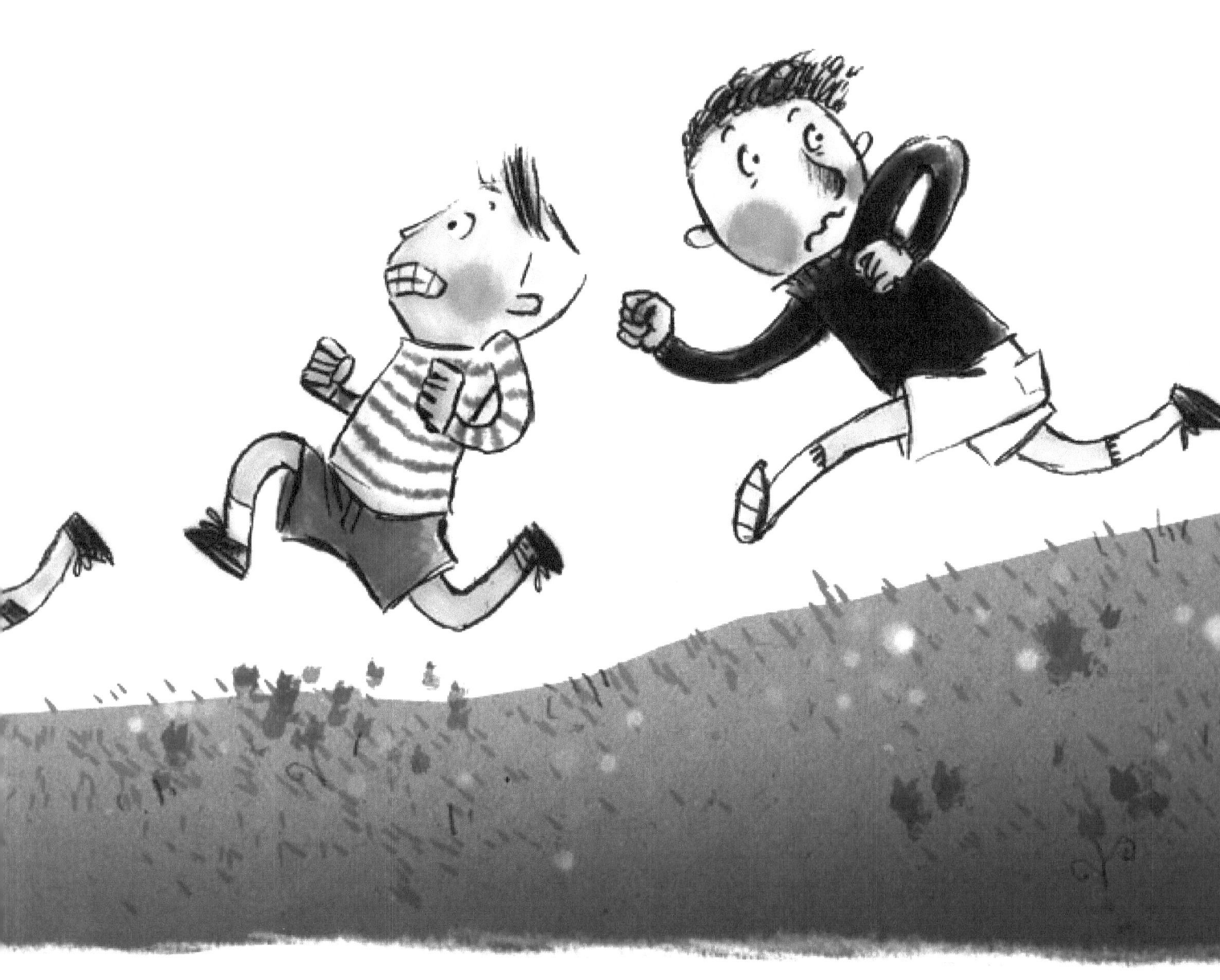

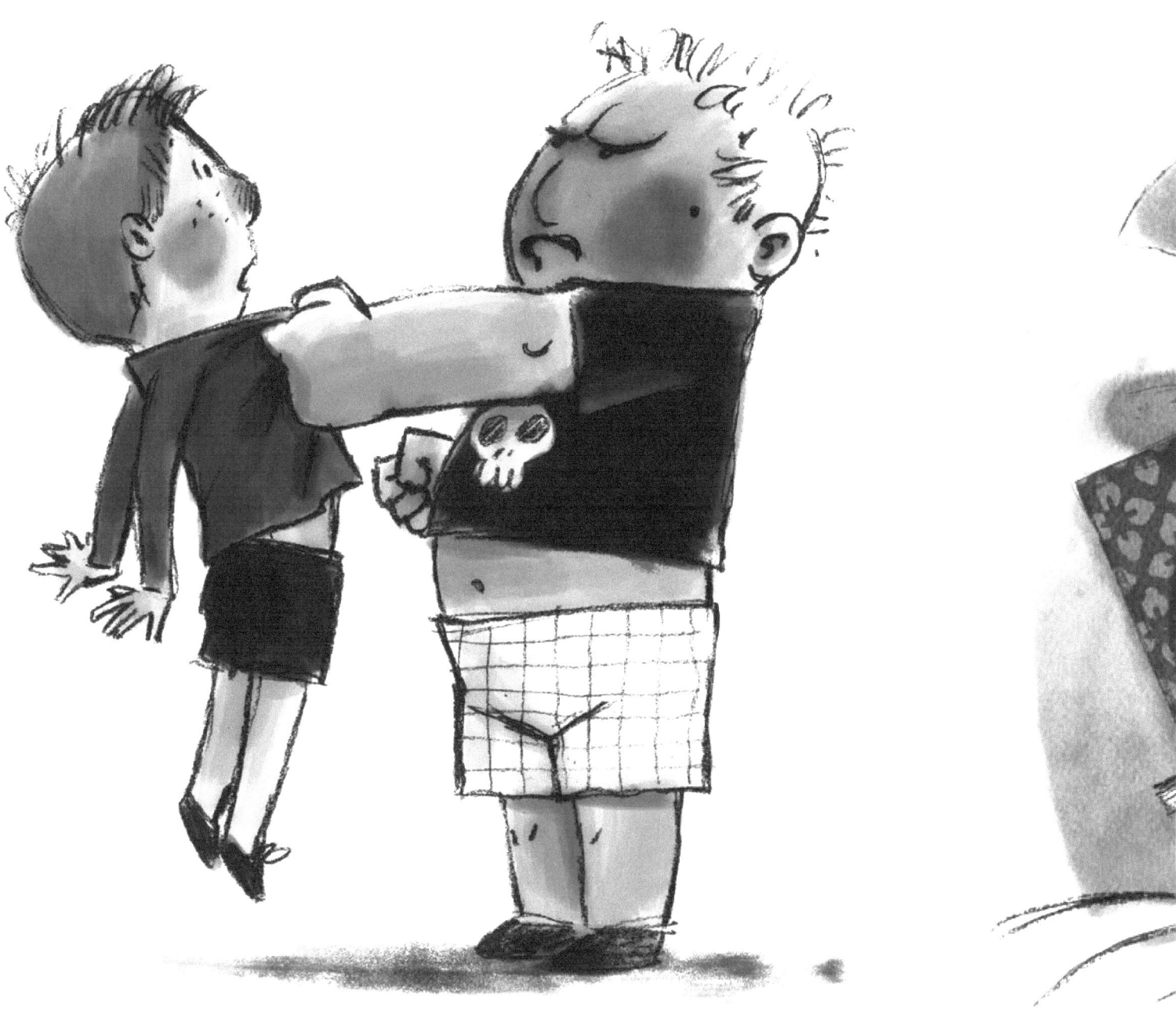

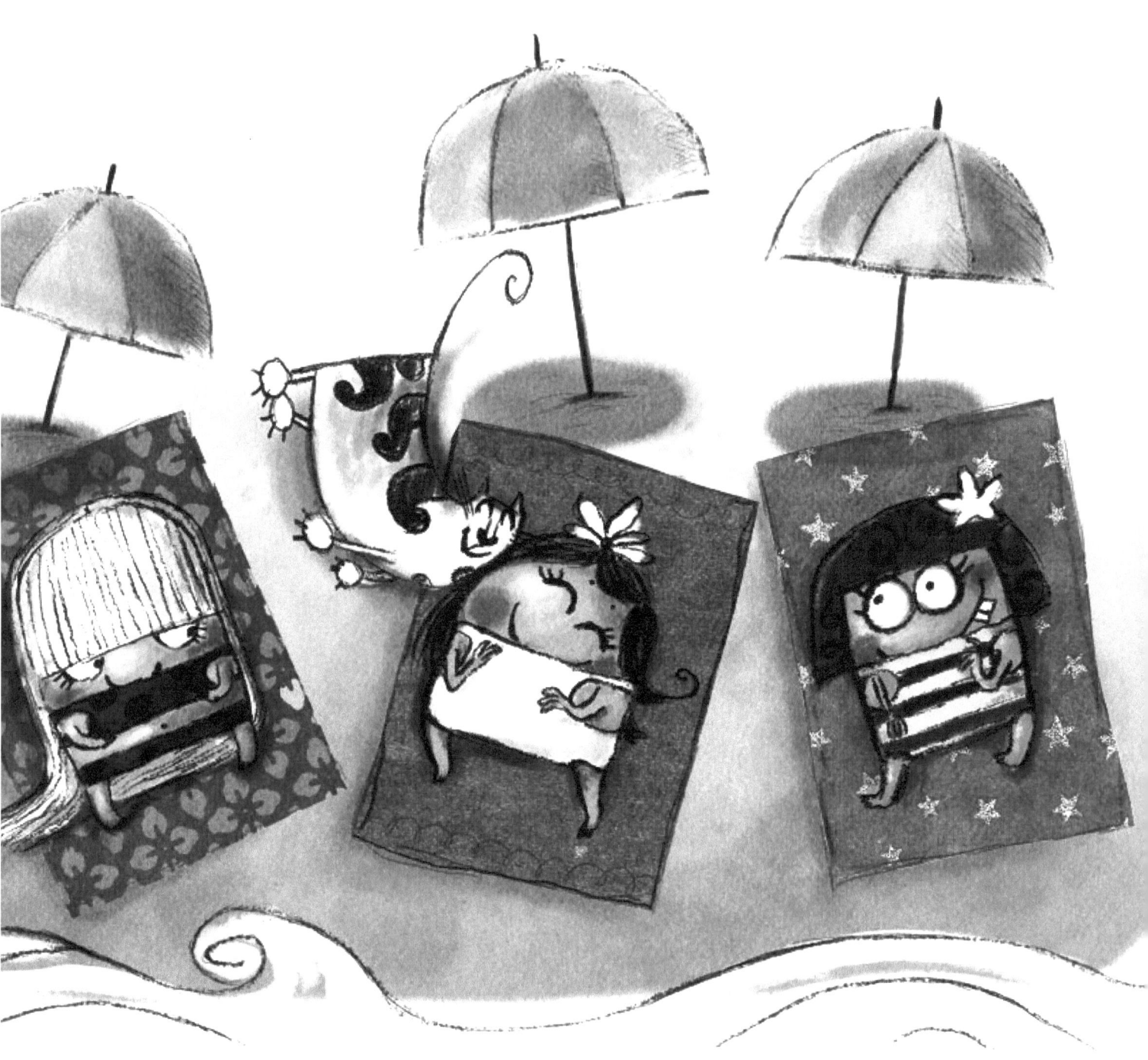

Artist:
Alexey Malina
Russia

URL:
www.makearea.com

Memories passing by
on the streets or maybe on the bridge's high
A moment of happiness
or an instant of sadness
Brings a bubbly smile,
else you are numb for a while
Desired or else ignored,
any of those;
but the memory gets stored.
constantly demanding action,
maybe for personal satisfaction,
ignoring or accepting is your decision,
what to do and what not is a big question
heart and mind go opposite in direction,
and if wanna stay out of this confusion
let the memory pass by without interruption.!!

Written by: Jigyasha

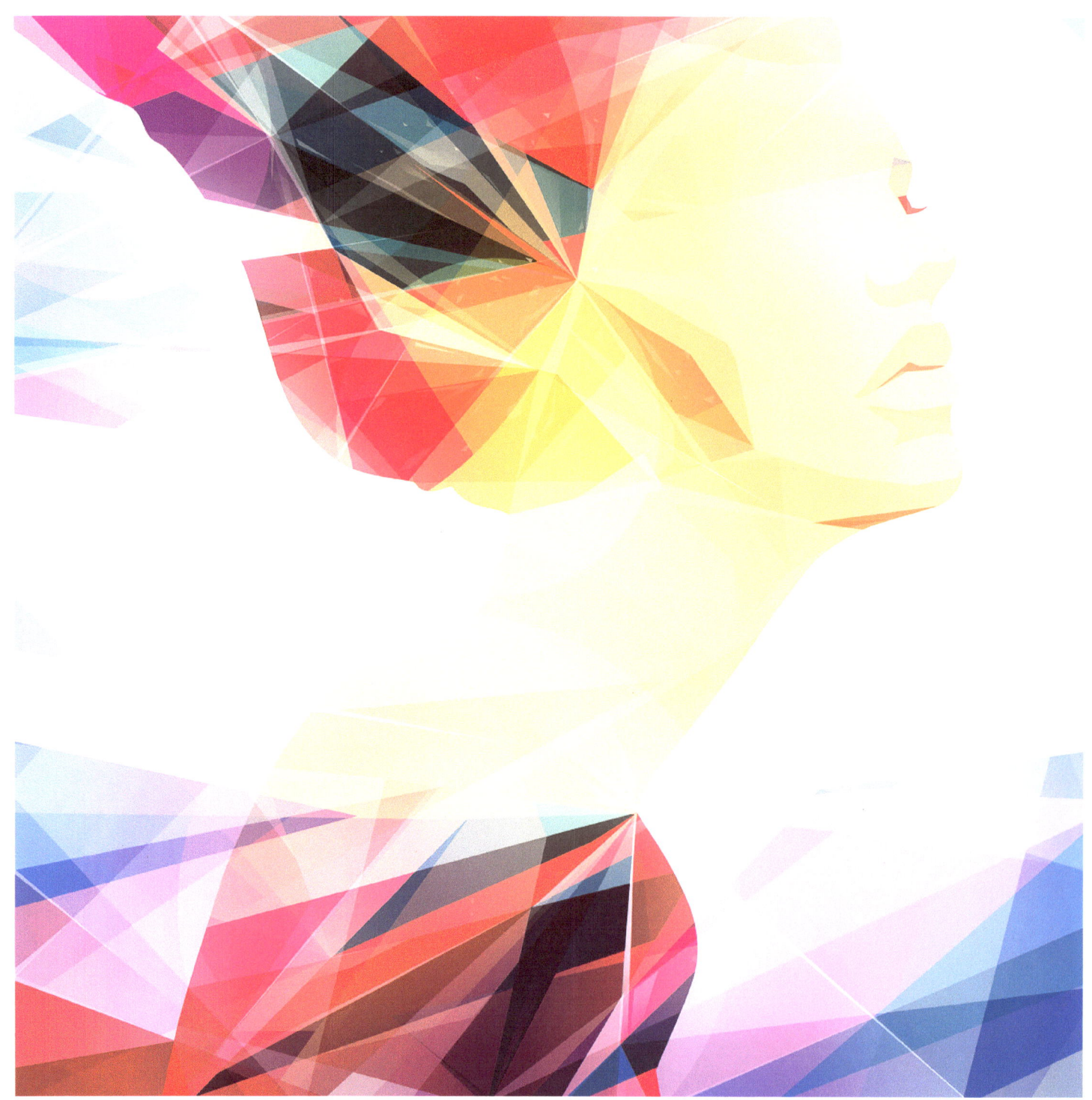

Non Cadenz

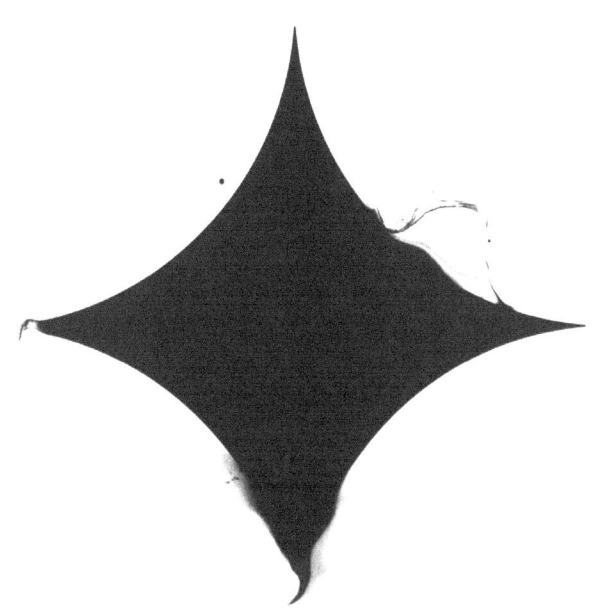

GREED

LU

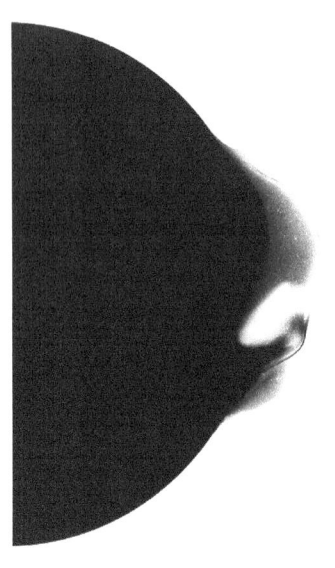

ST

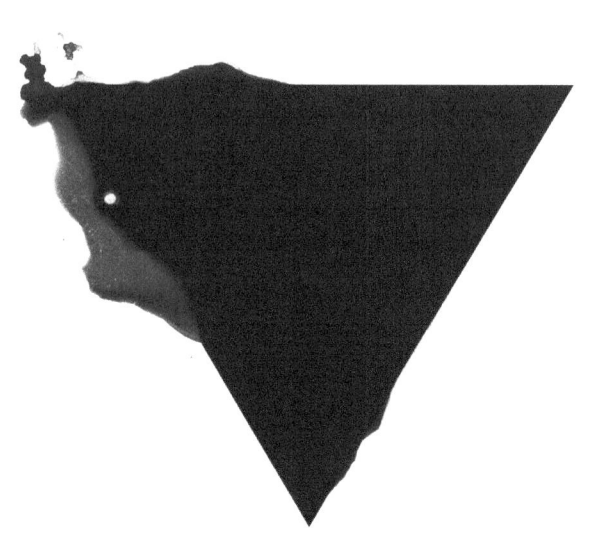

WRATH

Artist:
Anamaria Vîrlan
Romania

URL:
http://www.behance.net/anamariavirlan

From the moon's
soft light
a banana hangs
with roses and syrup
in a glass
full of hot coffee
with a ladder
climbing to the grapevine
from the interval of a movie
with pop corns losing
their way in kissed mouths
composed in his arm
your head leans
as if rivers were paradise
in the museum of love.

Written by: Nikhil Nath

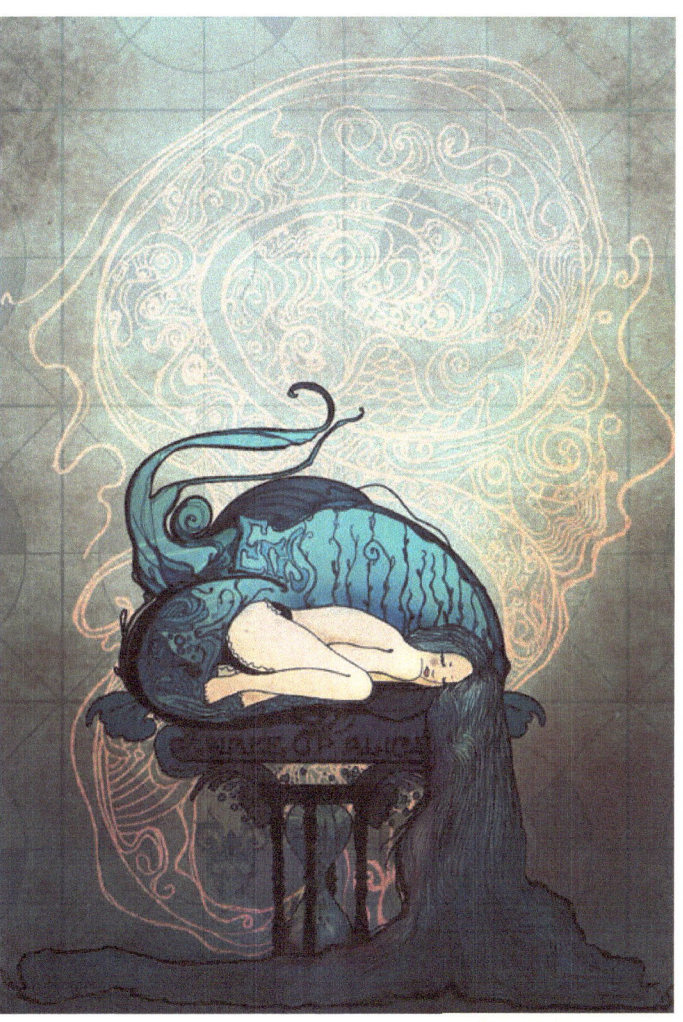

Wake up Alice

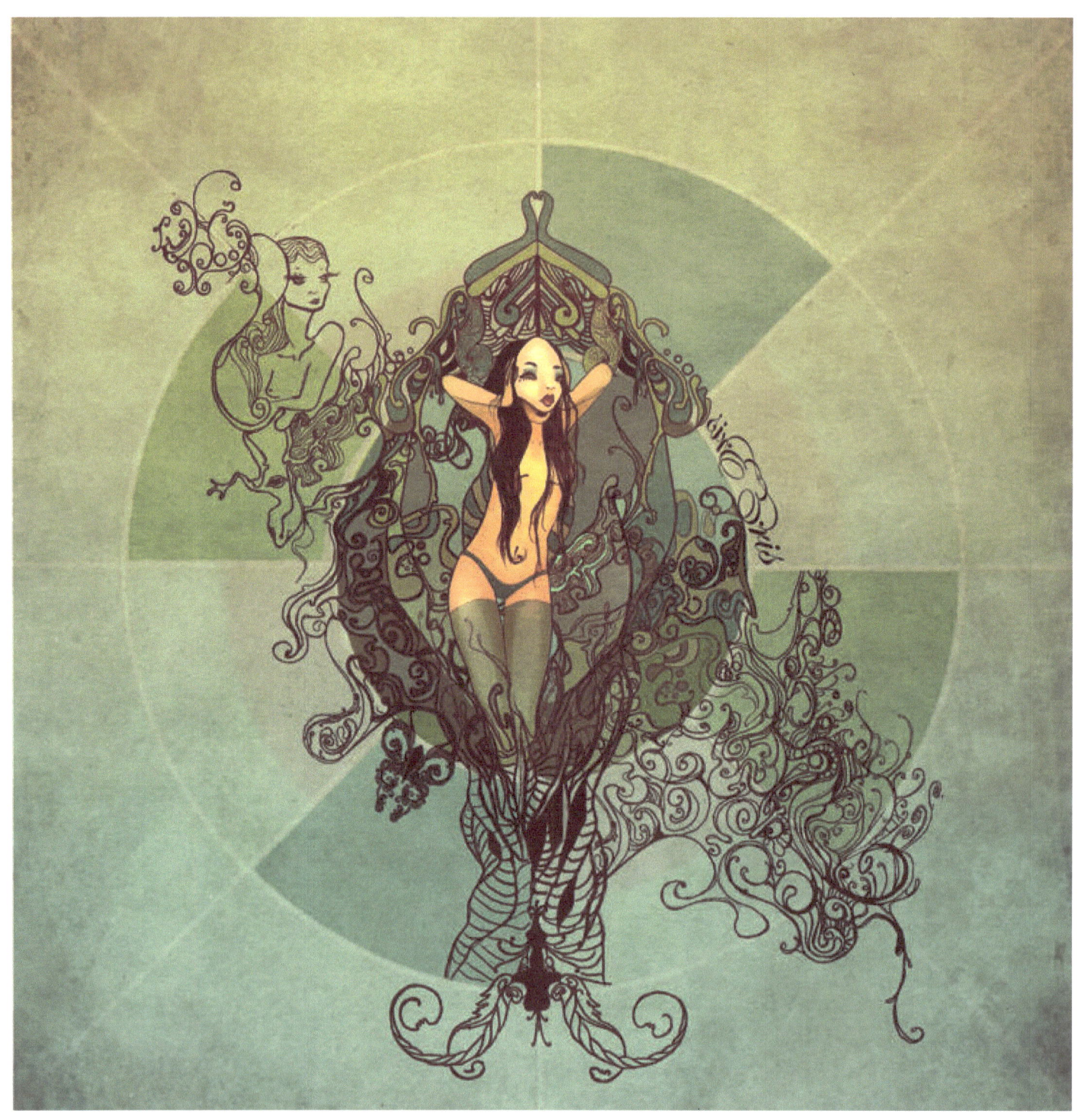

Artist:

Bixn
Austria (working in Spain)

URL:
www.birgitpalma.at

I may not have been
The perfect Mum
But this I have to tell
I will always to be there for you
Whether it is near or far
To lend a listing ear
Or give a hug
To wipe a tear and dry your eyes
But one thing I have to tell
Is my unconditional love for you
So when my time on earth is done
And I have gone to the heavens above
Please I ask you to remember
My unconditional Love for You
I won't go very far away
So when you are feeling down
And see a butterfly
Or a star shining brightly in the sky
Then you will know
That it will be me
With my unconditional love For You.

Written by: June McAnoy

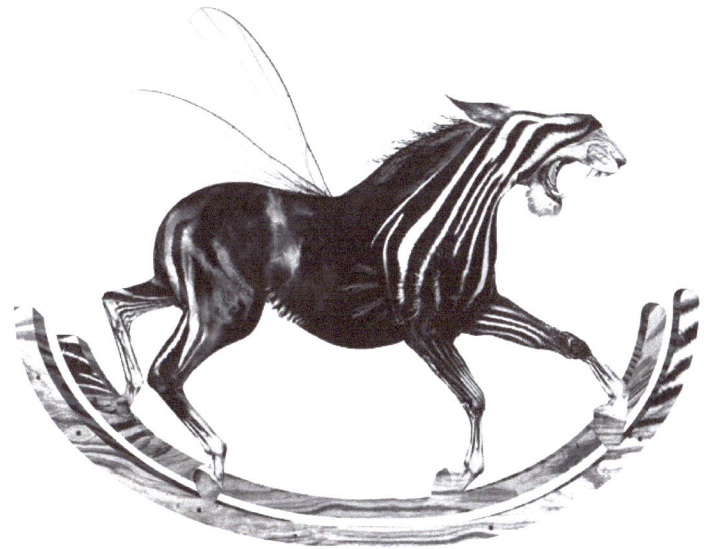

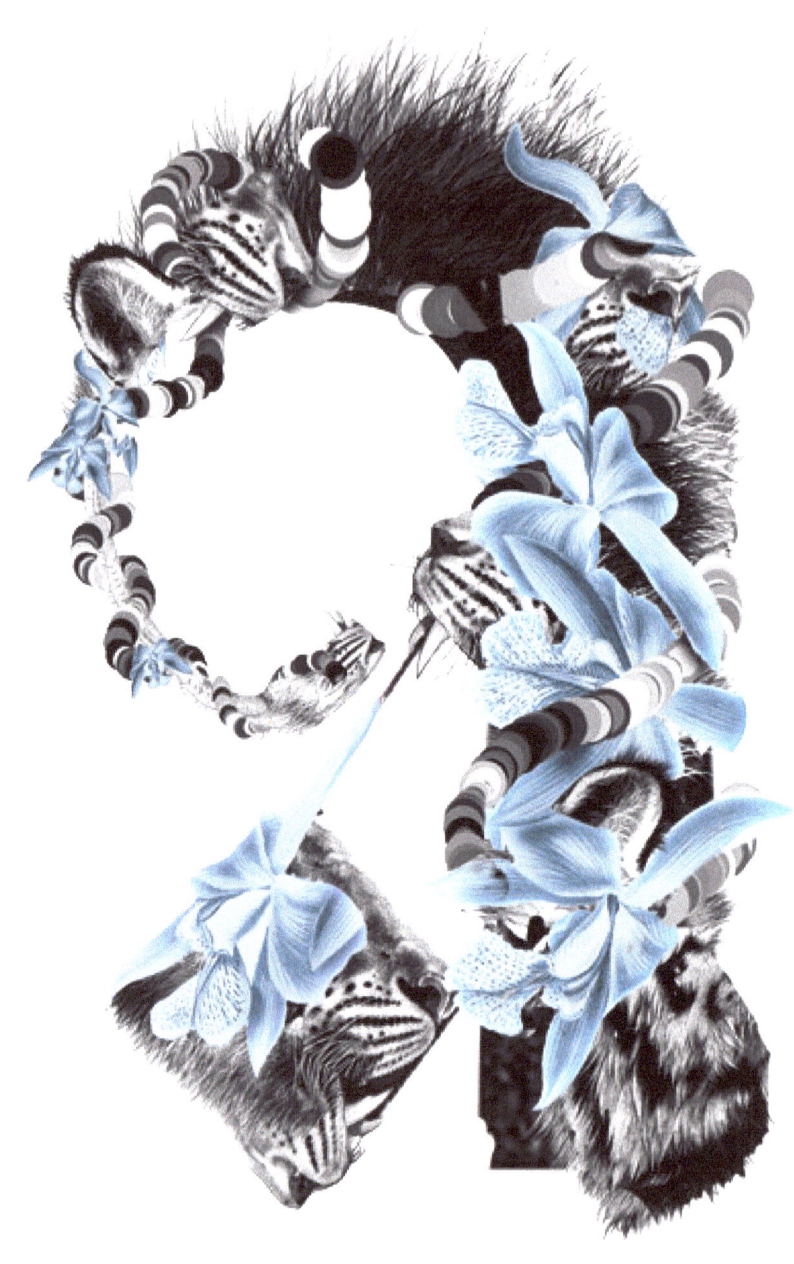

Only A's allowed.

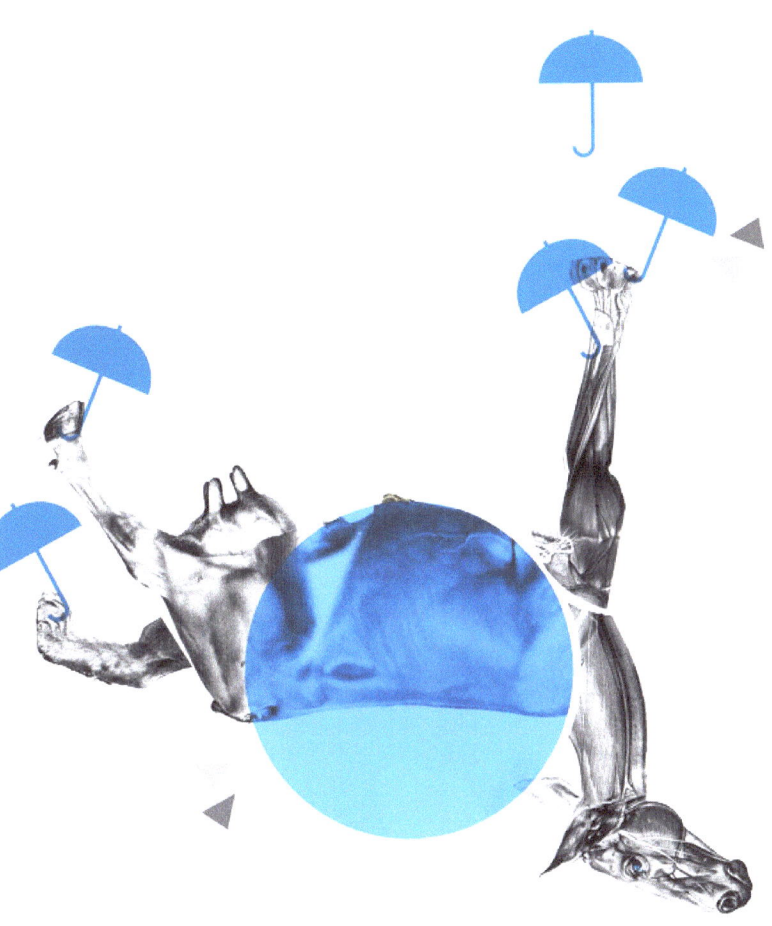

Free Falling.

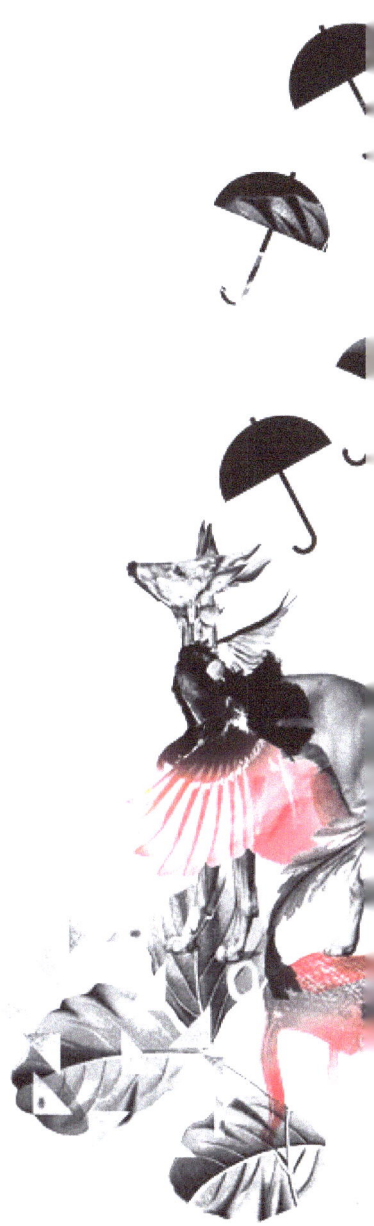

Grow u

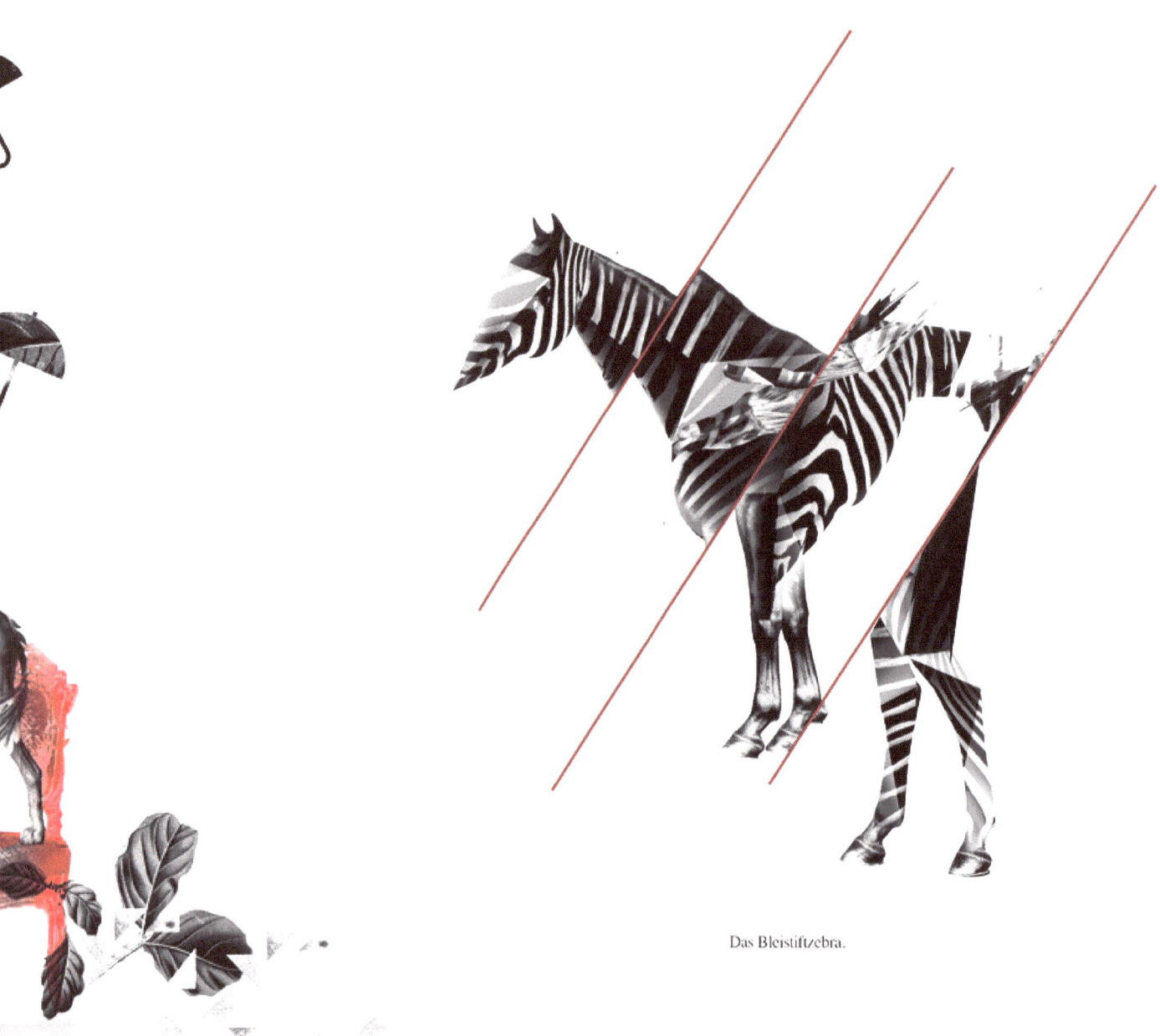

Das Bleistiftzebra.

p.

Artist:
Claudio Parentela
Italy

URL:
http://www.claudioparentela.net

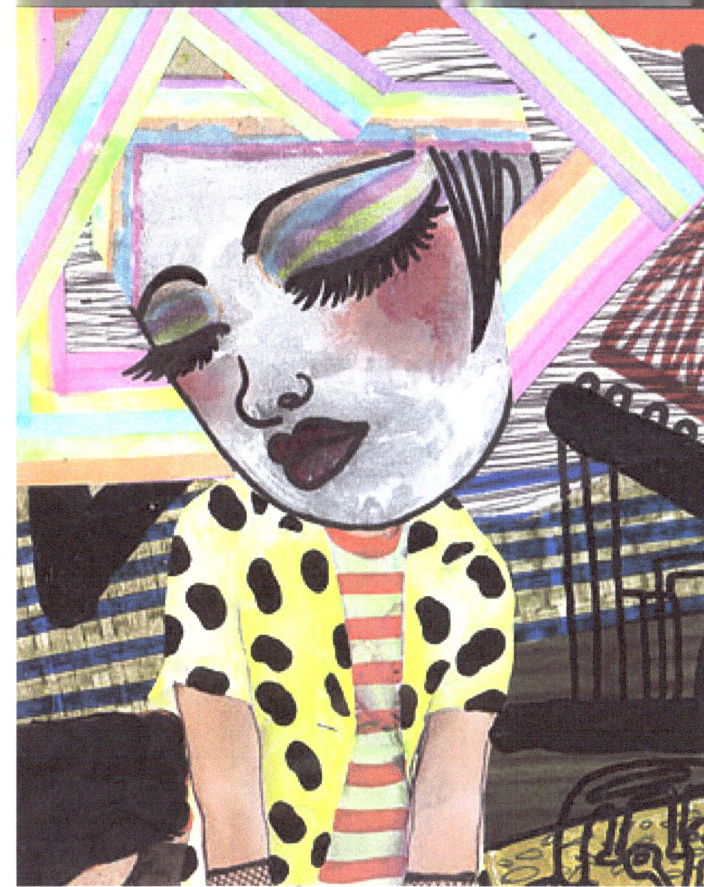

Grumpy the clown wore a terrible frown,
he had nothing to be happy about
He had no money or friends to play with
and never would have no doubt
Then one day whilst making his way
through a dark and silent wood
He spotted a face, such a horrible face,
and there petrified he stood
He stood for an hour not daring to move
trying to look brave and tall
He stood for an hour and then realised
that the face hadn't moved at all
So he moved just a bit and then he was hit
with the truth that was plain to see
That face is no face, that face is my face,
that face is Grumpy, that's me
Then a fish broke the water and started his laughter
which hasn't stopped to this day
And as a result he now is happy
and has friends with which to play.

Written by: John Mullan

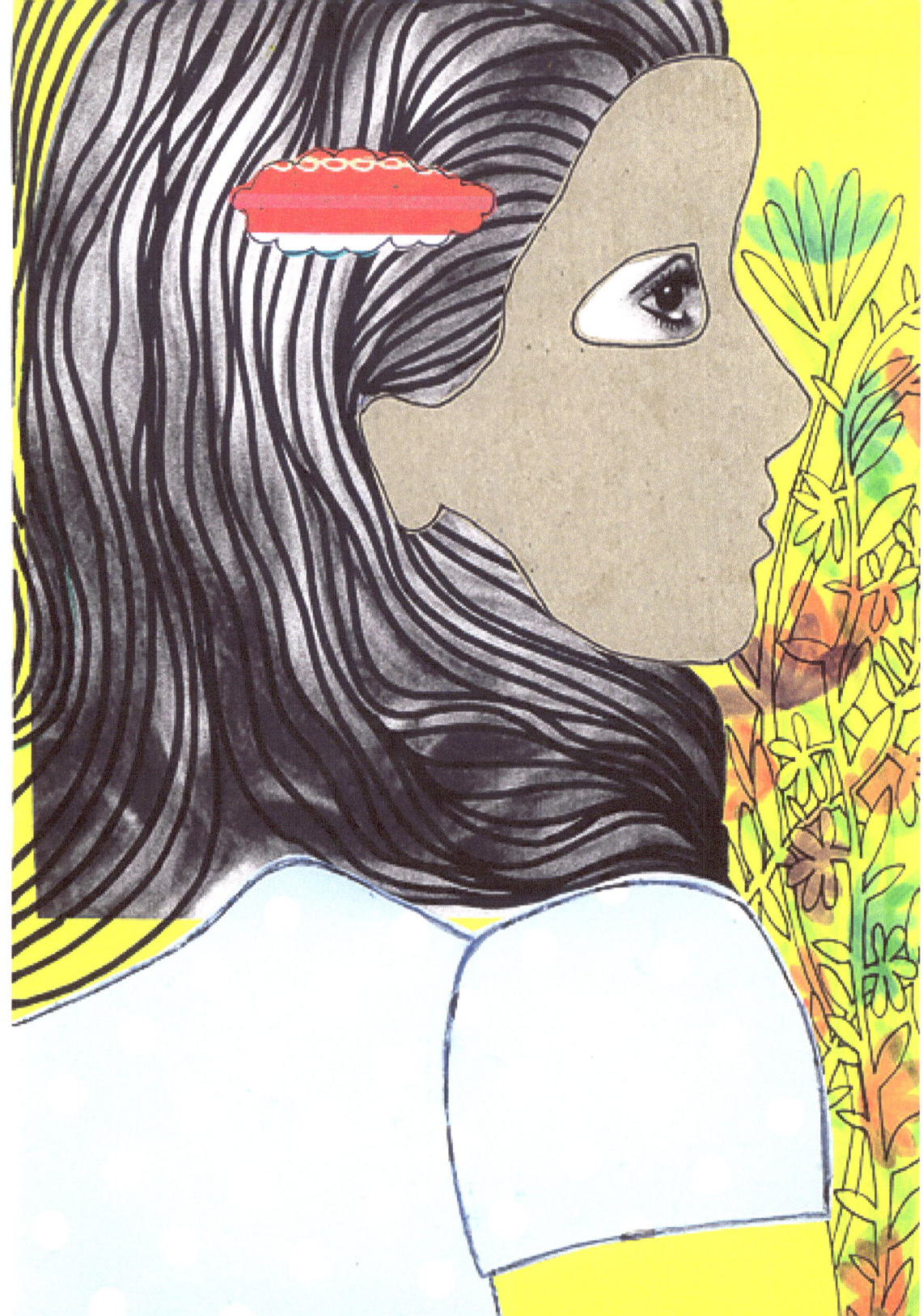

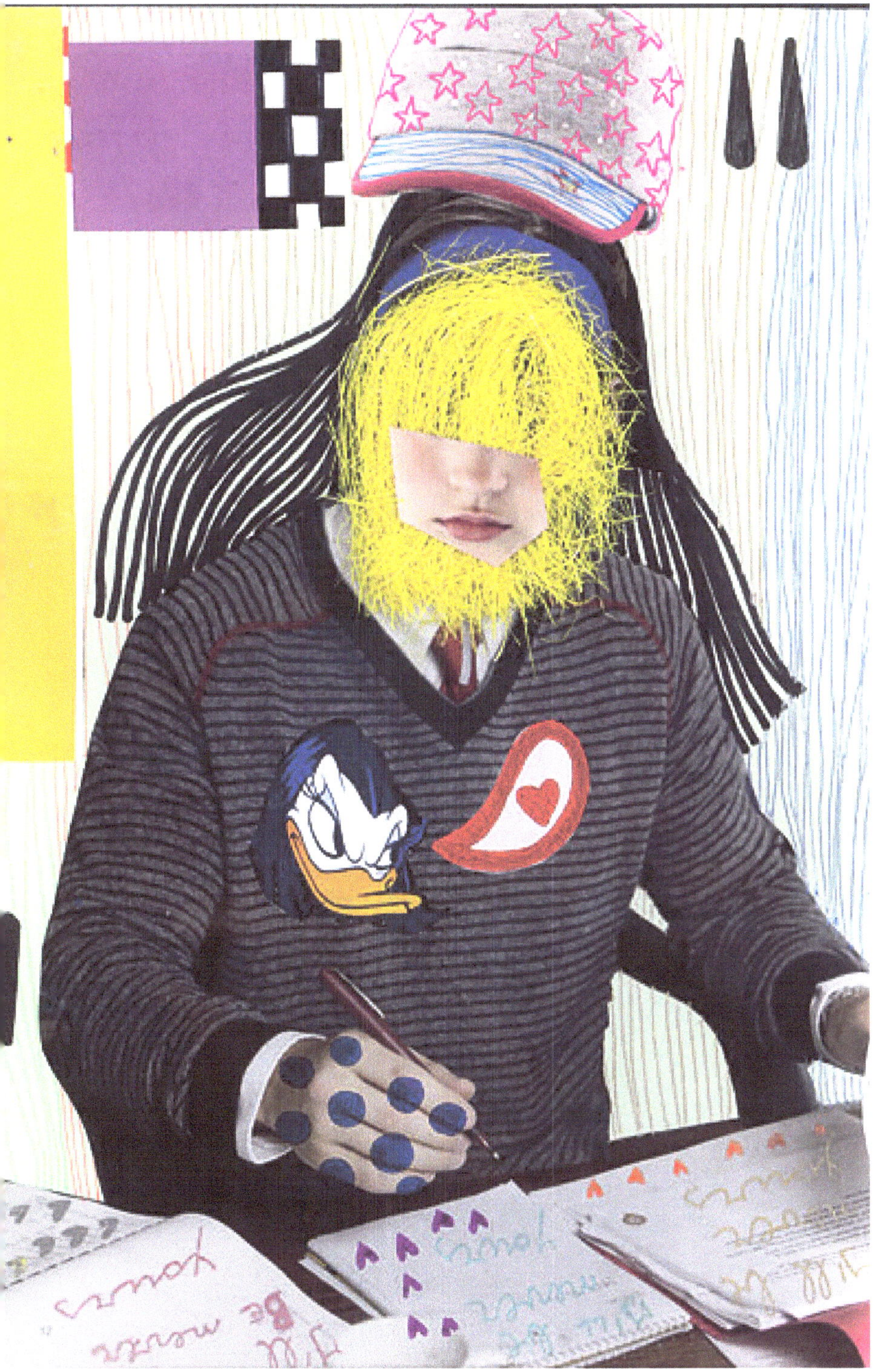

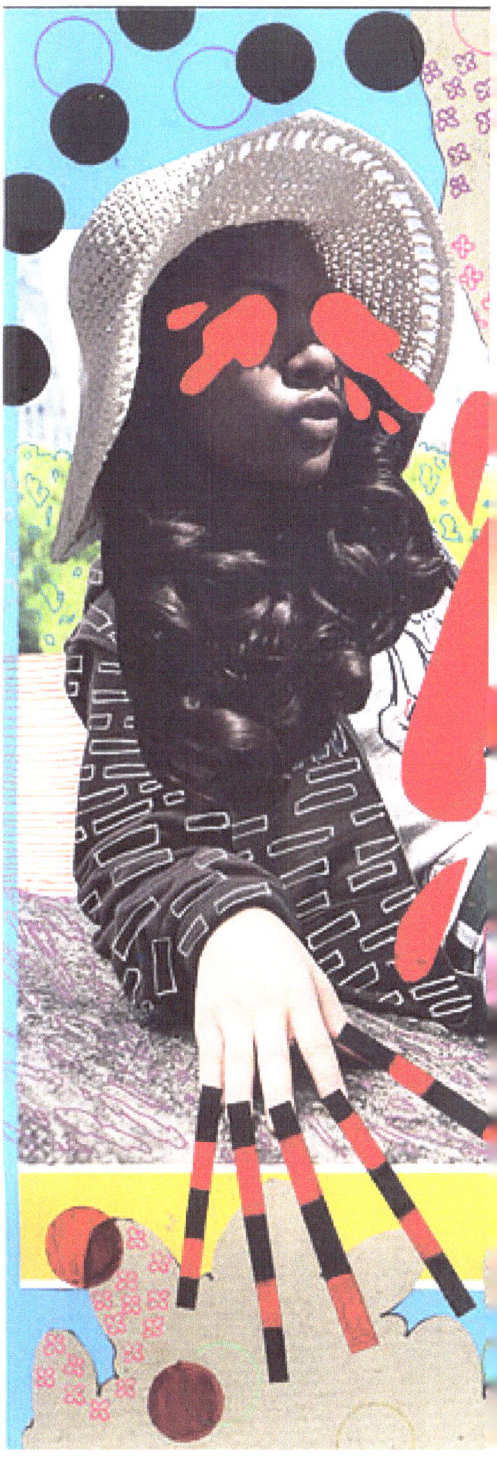

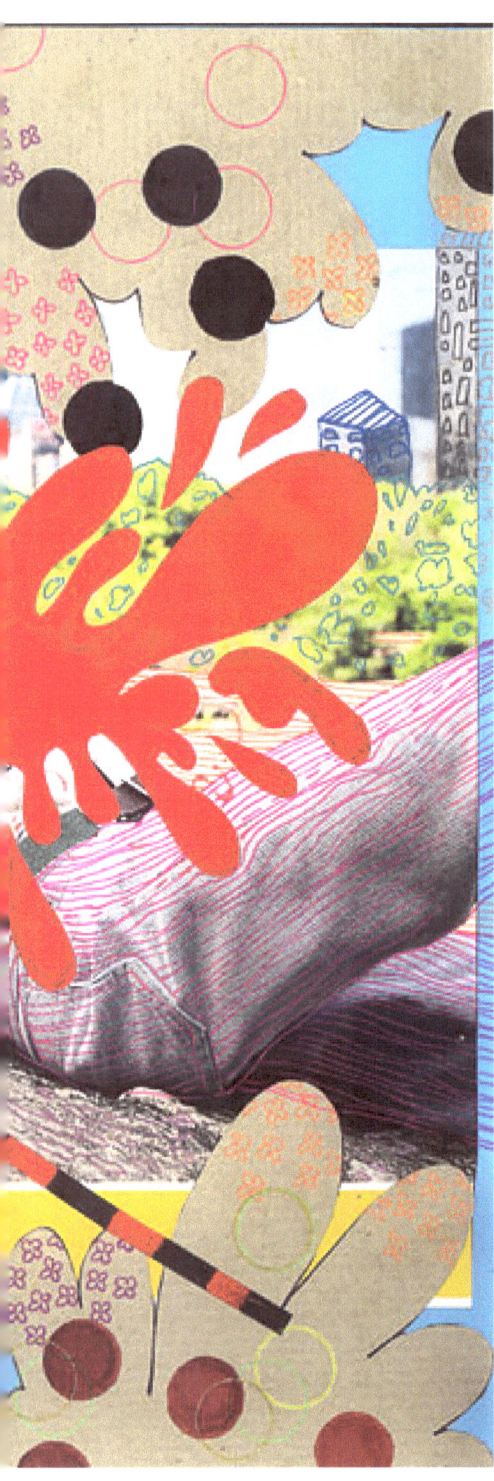

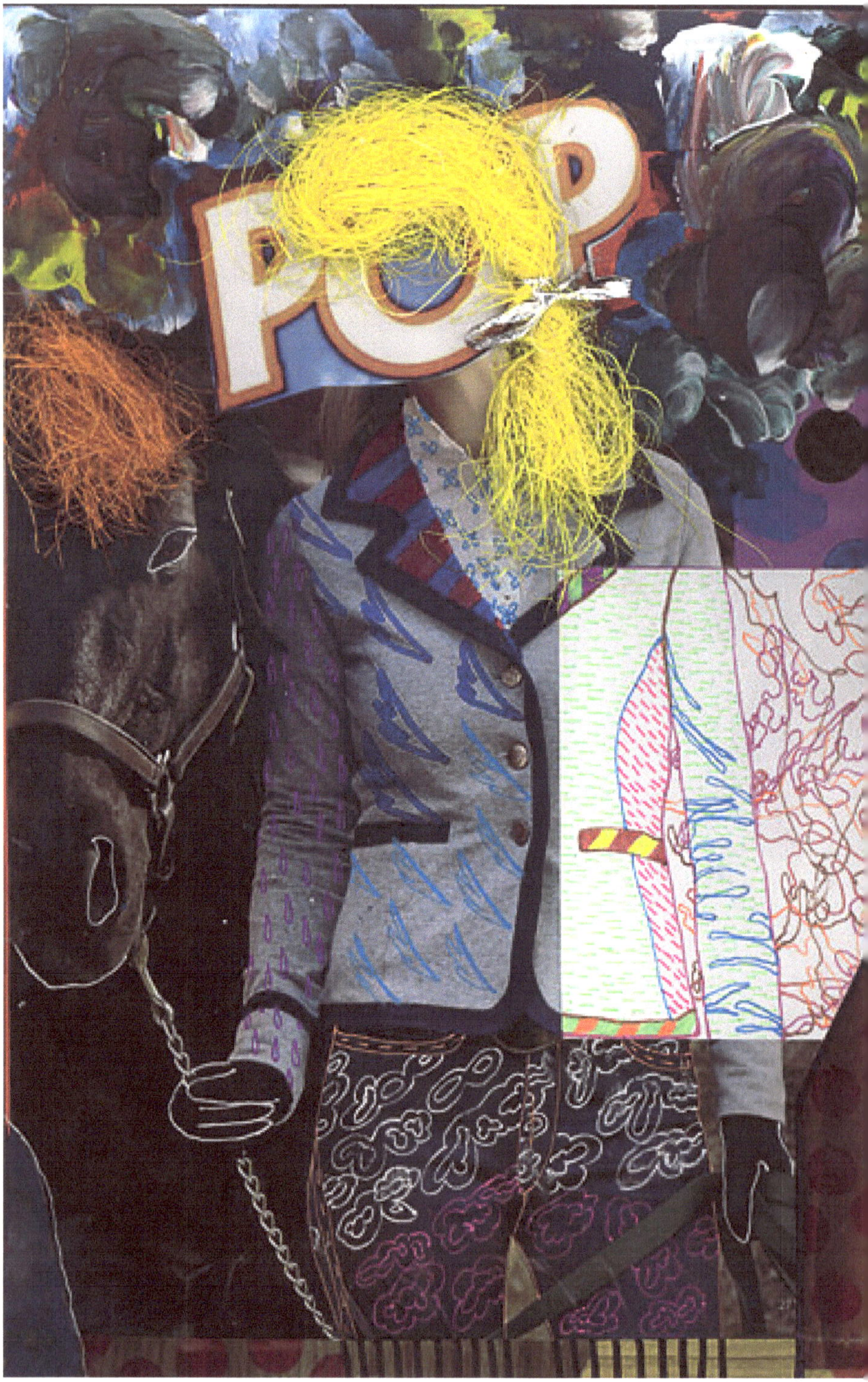

Artist:
Christopher Crawford
United kingdom

URL:
http://www.crawforddesigns.co.uk

One magnificent night,
With a man worth to fight;
A man like a prophet,
His words I can't forget.

A Chance to endeavour,
The one I might been dreaming for.
Your Greatness I can savour;
Certainly! The one I am looking for.

Lonely night I long,
Your dazzling blue eyes caught me on.
Please! Don't get me wrong:
But you turns me on.

Peculiar myths to say
It's you I swear and pray.
I may sound like crazy,
But its you I can dance with baby!

Just give it a try,
I assure you ain't gonna cry.
One sudden night,
One sign of never ending light.

Written by: Carlos Castro jr.

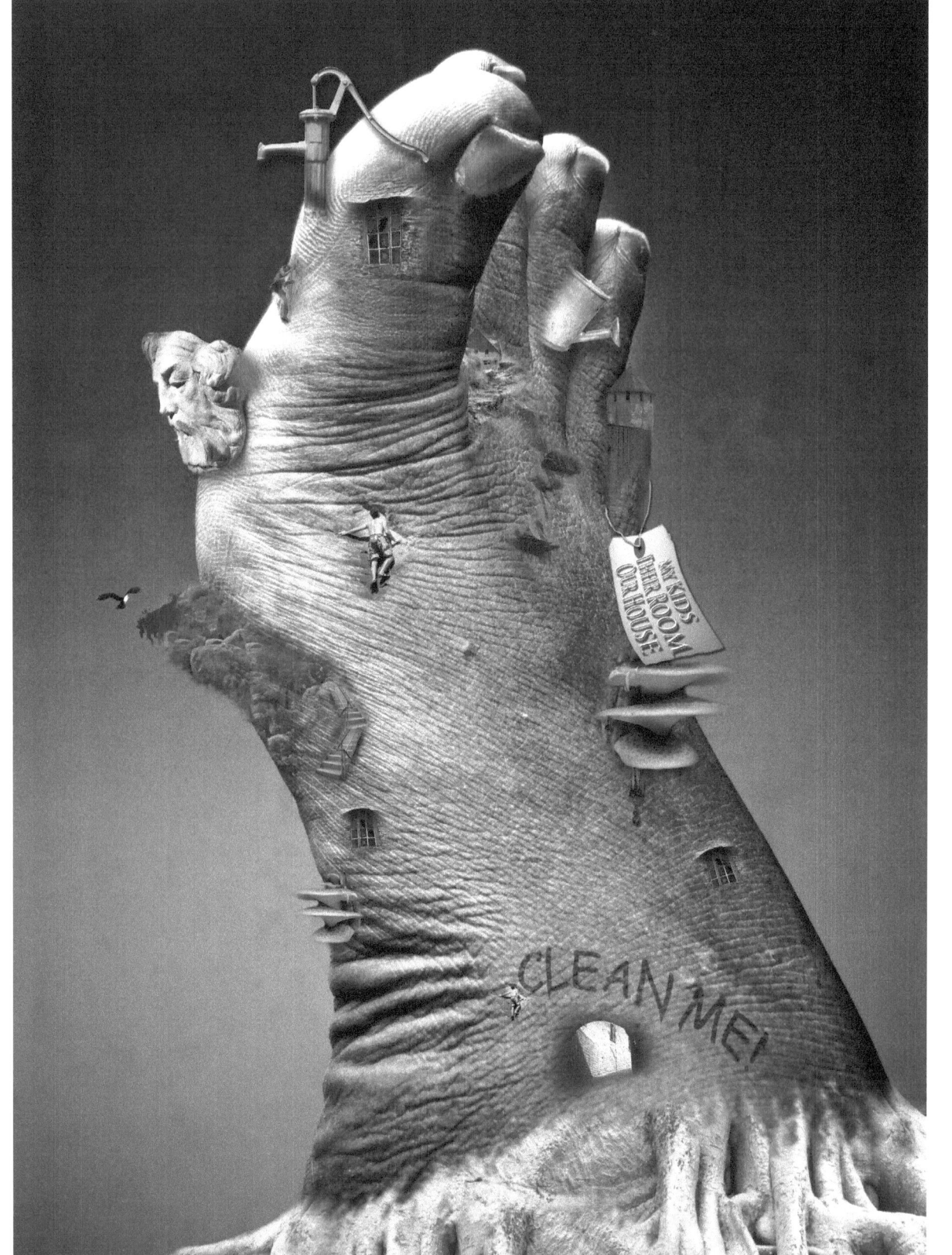

Clean M

Artist:
Jope
Spain

URL:
www.website.com

You, Who tamed me with lies
For no reason why
I know someday we'll have our own lives
As time passes by, I ask my self why?

Yes! I should accept,
It's you I cannot forget.
I'm scared and i hope you care,
Coz i have no one, but you i stare.

Thanks for all the deeds,
It lifts me far beyond those creeds.

I'll be miss'n You,
So sad but true.
I might droppin a clue,
But someday I'll find You.

Written by: Carlos Castro jr.

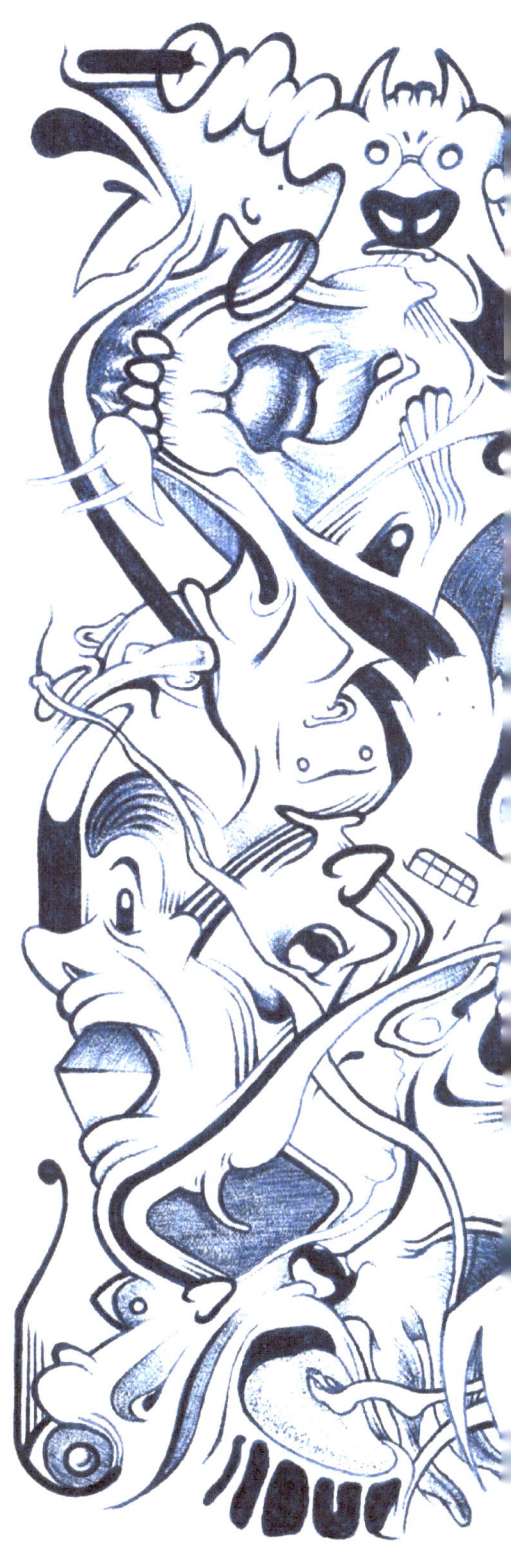

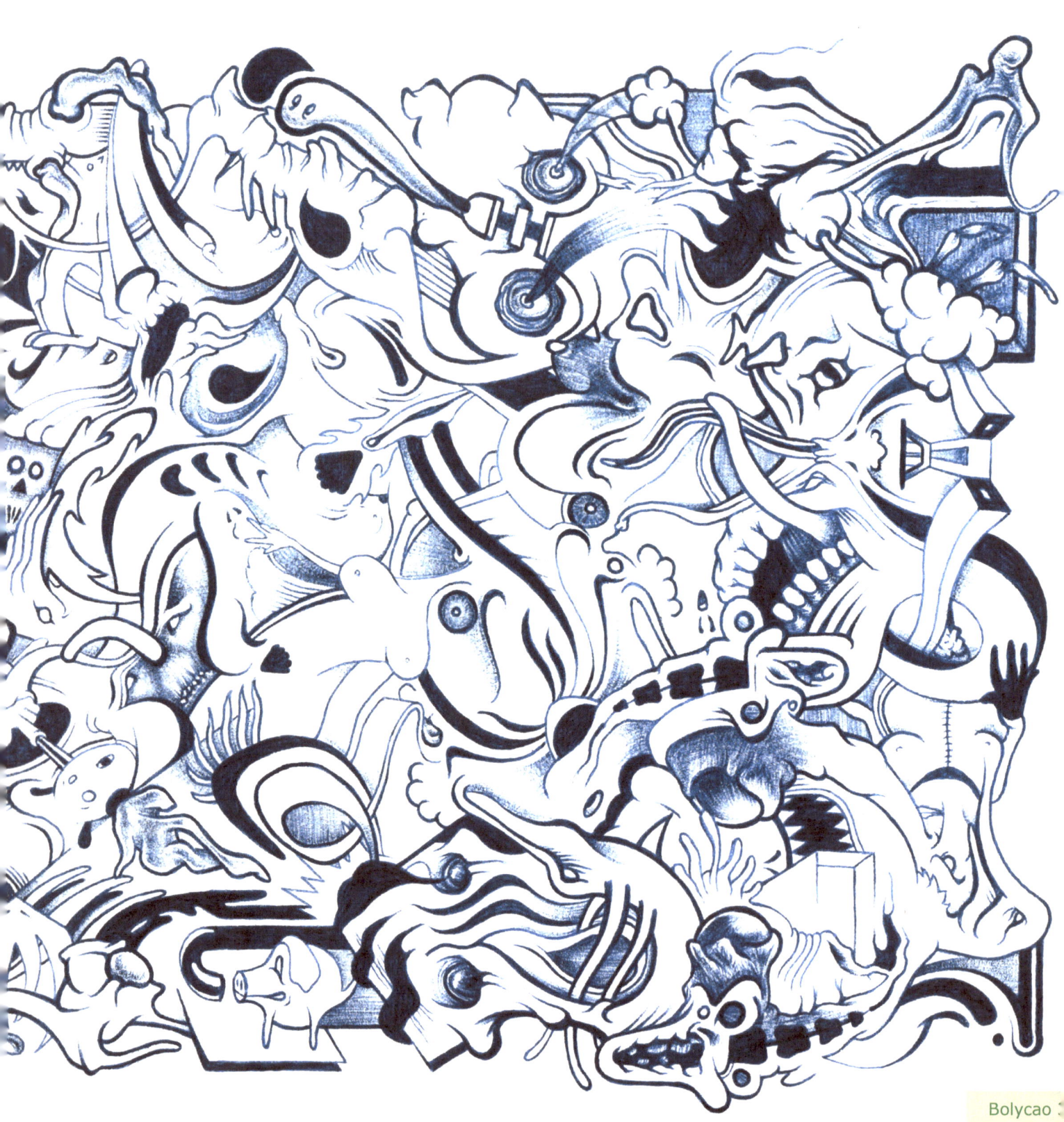

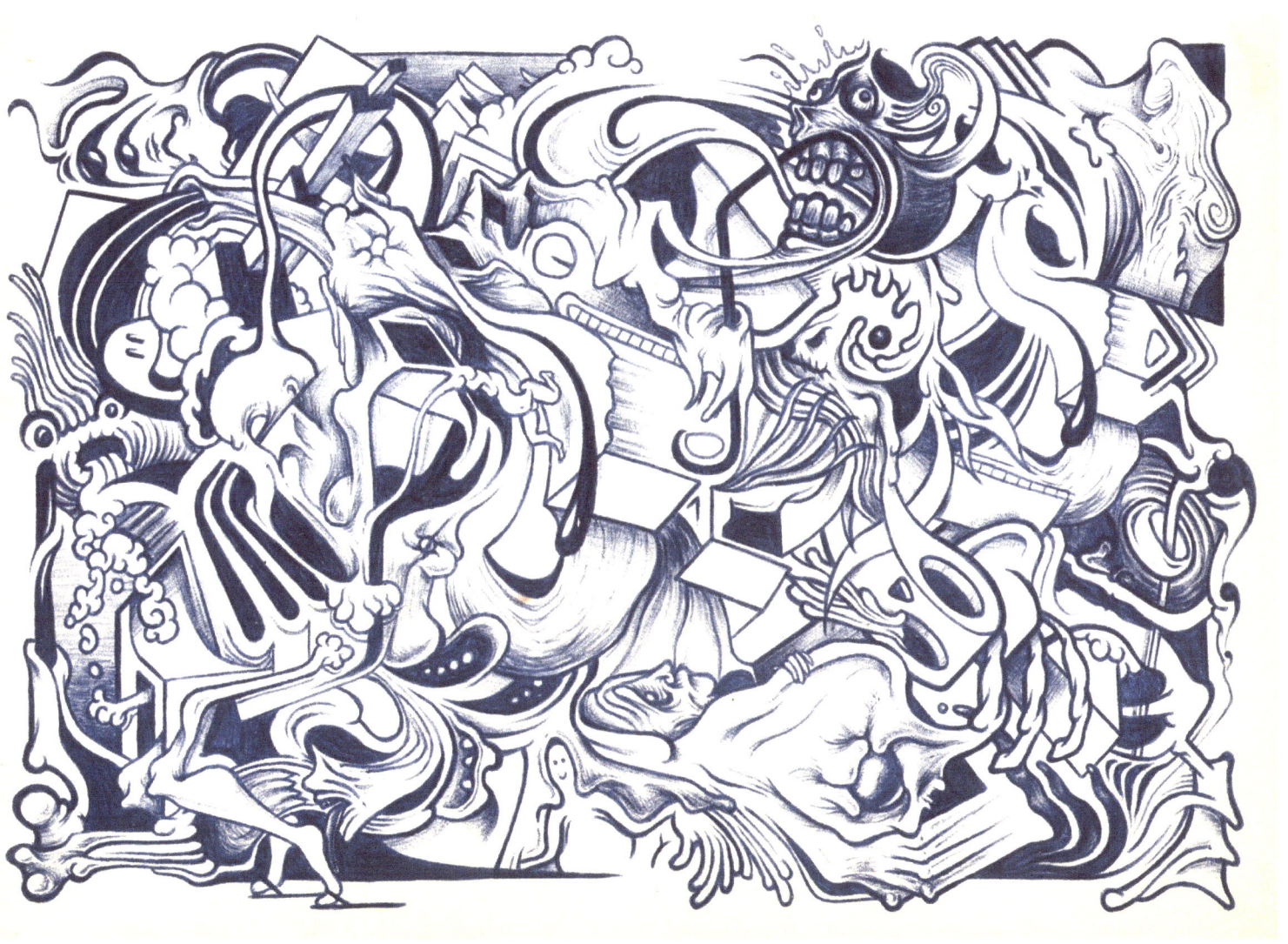

ycao 1

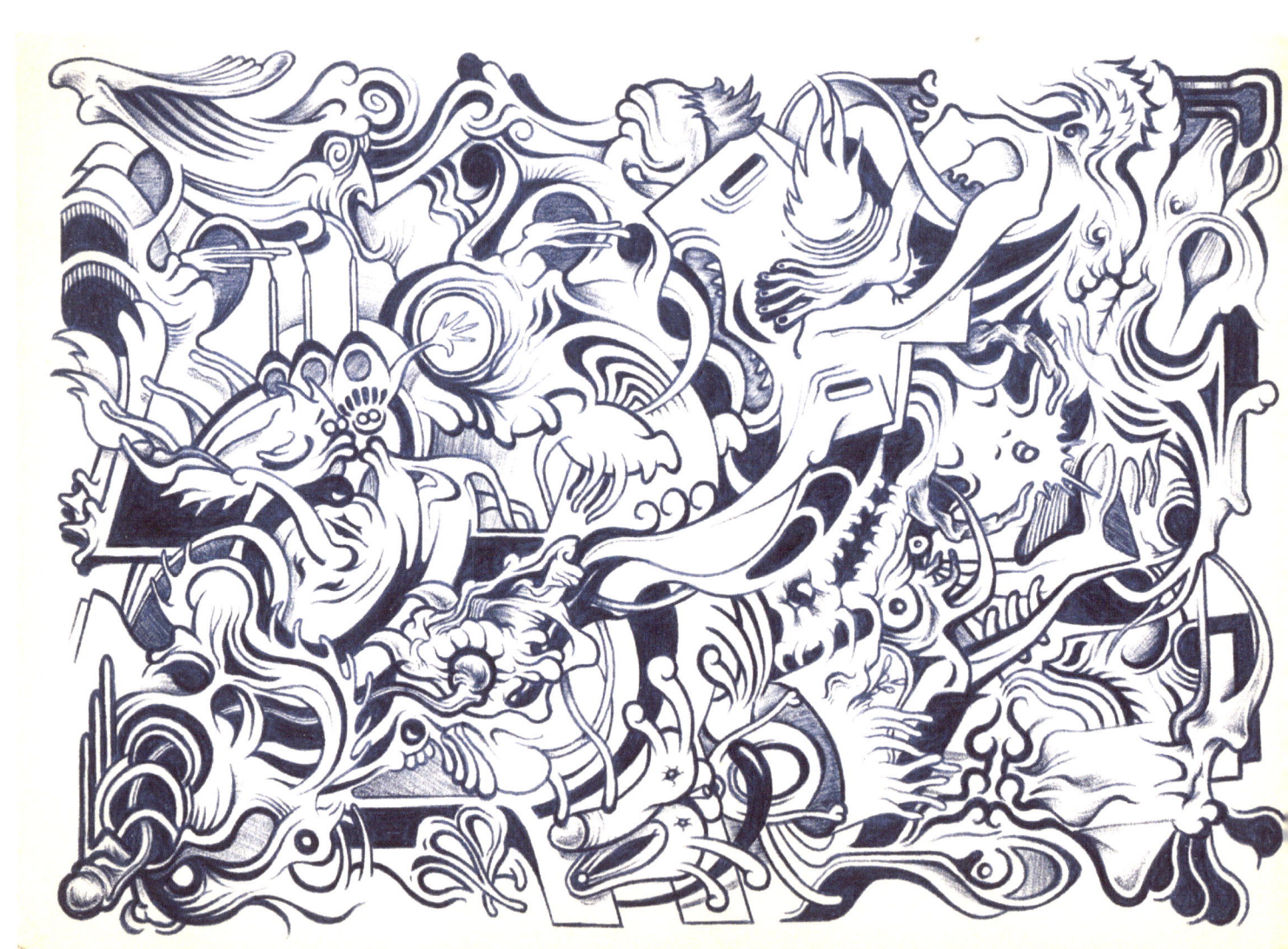

Bolyca

Artist:
Juan Manuel Tavella
Argentina

URL:
www.lagranepoca.com

From the symphony of sunlight
bedazzled in the rumor
a gossip falls on the North Pole
like a longitude of adventure
with no rain forecast
the yellow bike goes screaming
past the hilly road
chasing an avalanche of embargo
in the ship of a flower less empire.

Written by: Nikhil Nath

Leonard Cohen

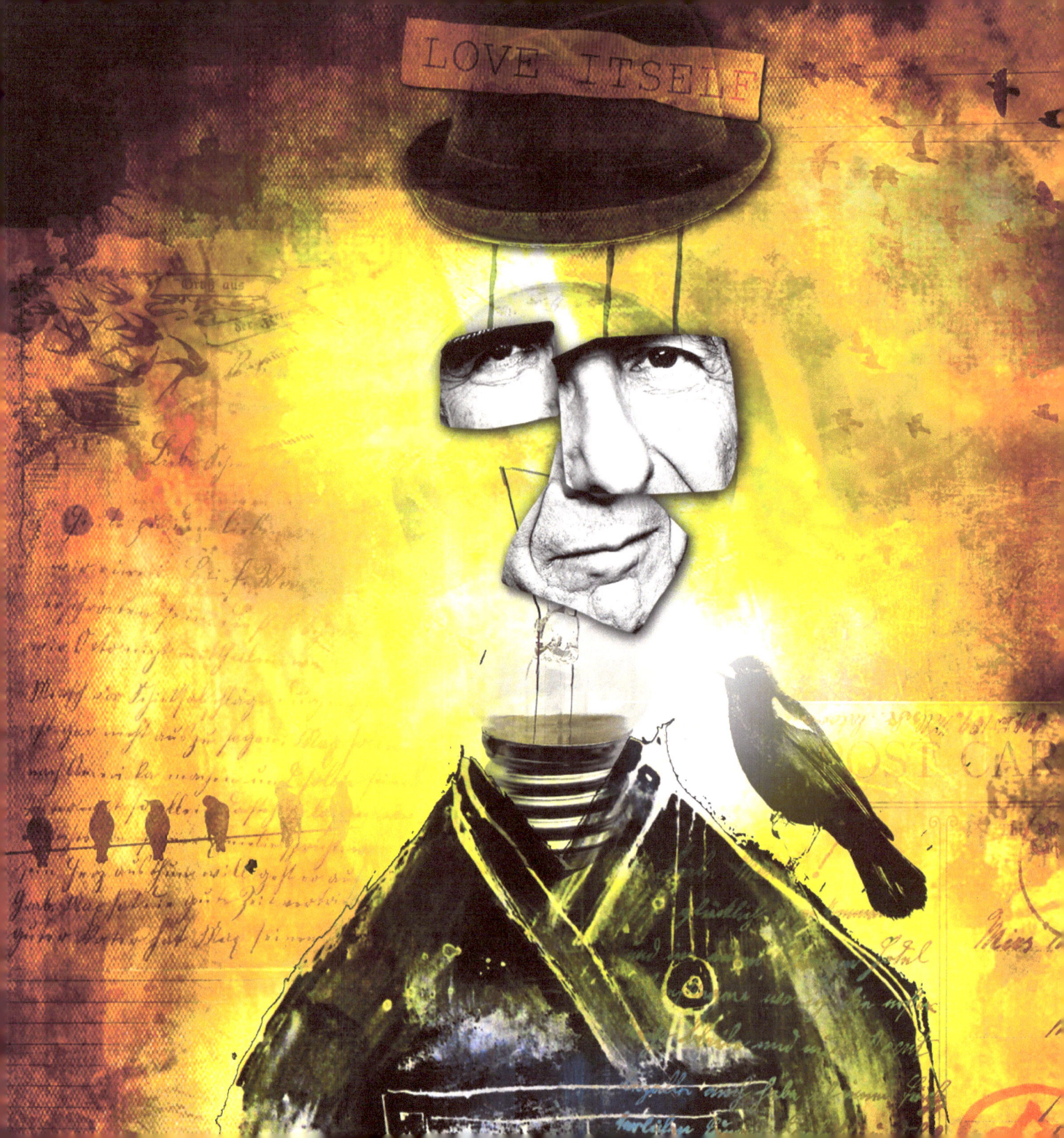

Artist:
Labate Saccol
Argentina

URL:
http://labatesaccol.blogspot.com/

I set out observant, to find myself
Beyond the dogmatic sea Headstrong,
sober I flew the vicious shore
Angelic hope,guiding me
I felt the antagonistic skeptic
Call me from behind a cloud
The voice burned, irrational, to the core
Passion no longer allowed
I lost all pretty before i hit ground
Love and devotion tossed in wind
For new freedom I had found
I will take this flight again
With her spirit, faultless, constant
I breathe I call for her and she still hears
True devotion never leaves
And grows throughout the years.

Written by: Lanny Wafer

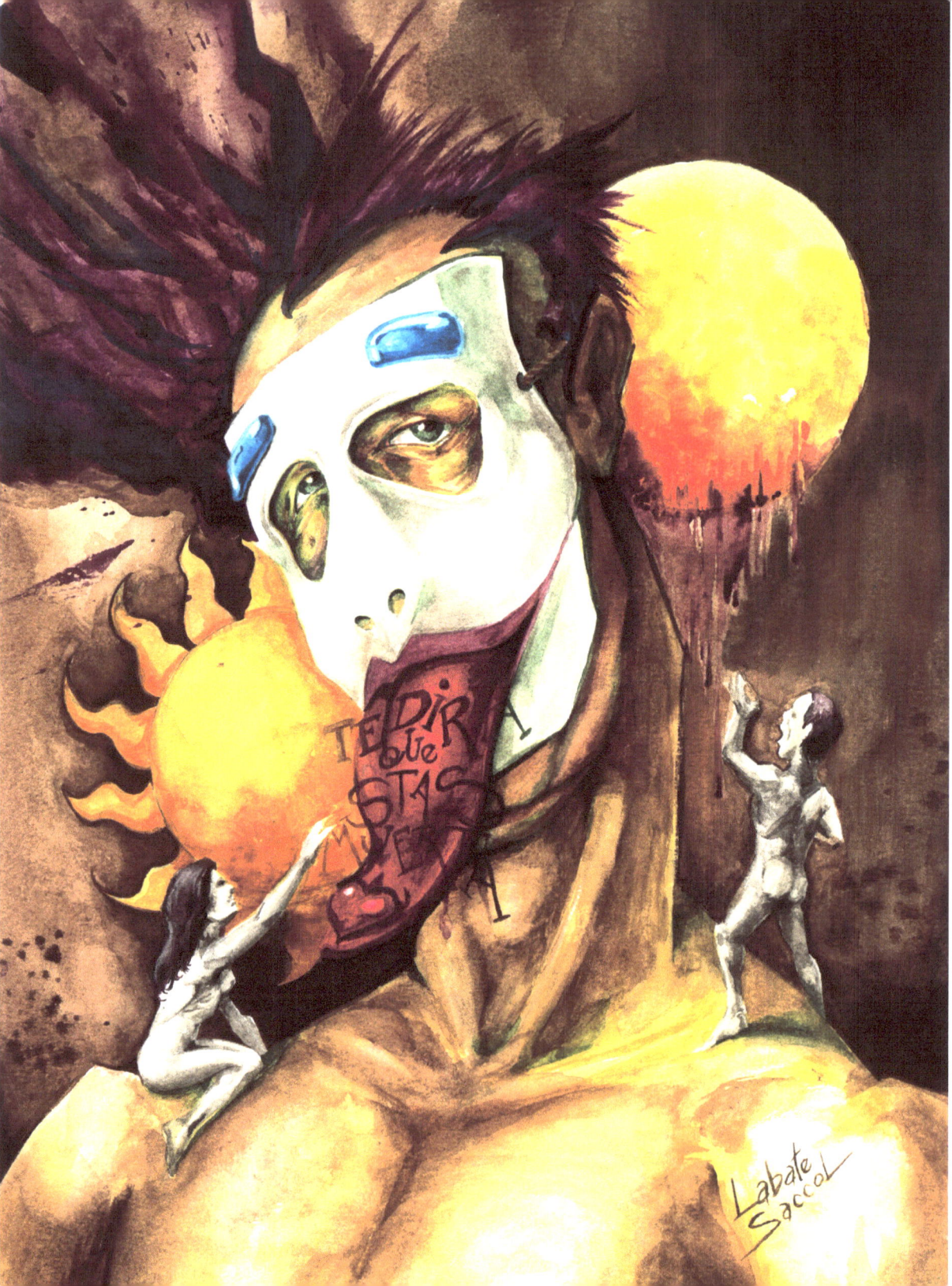

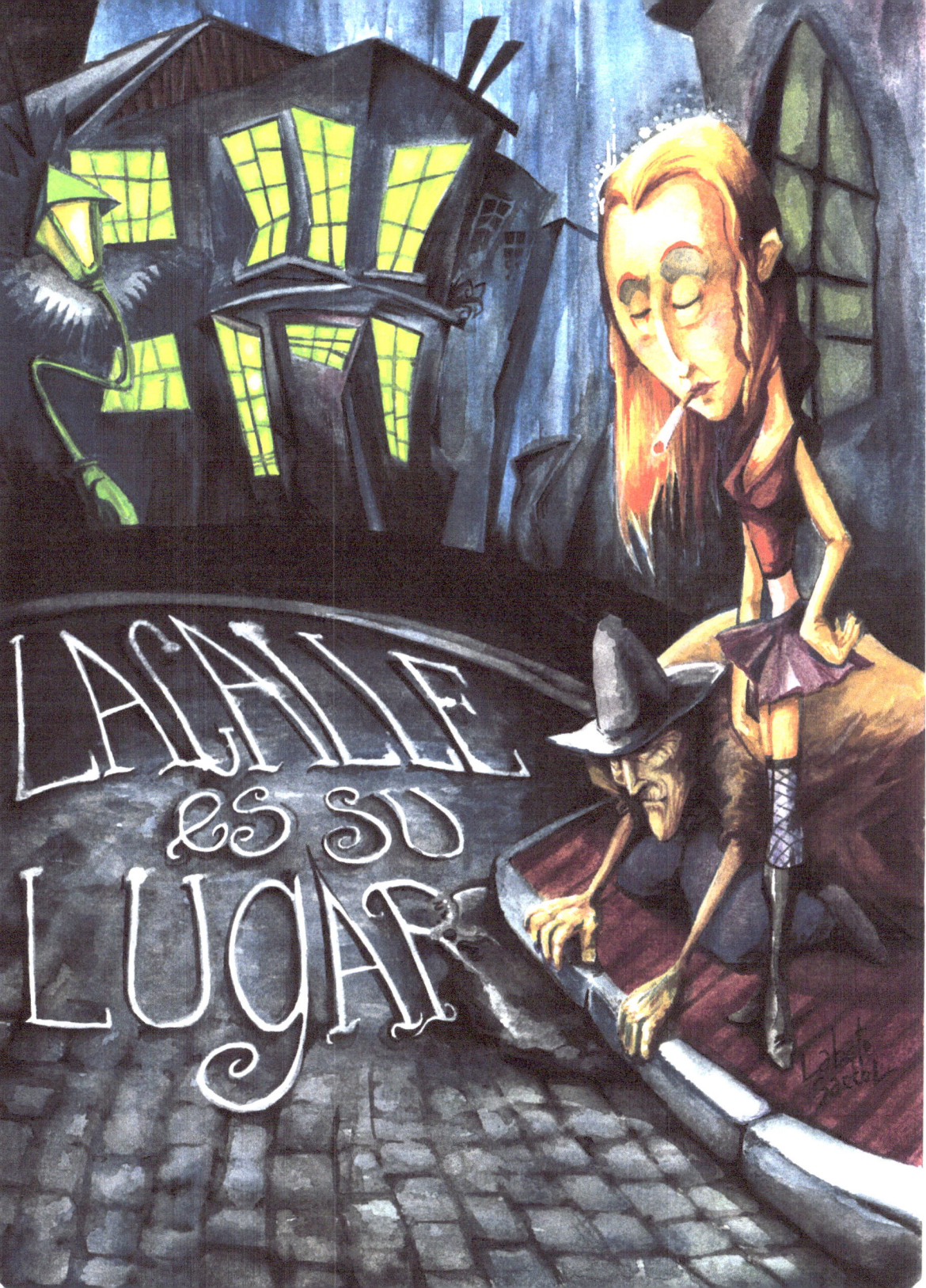

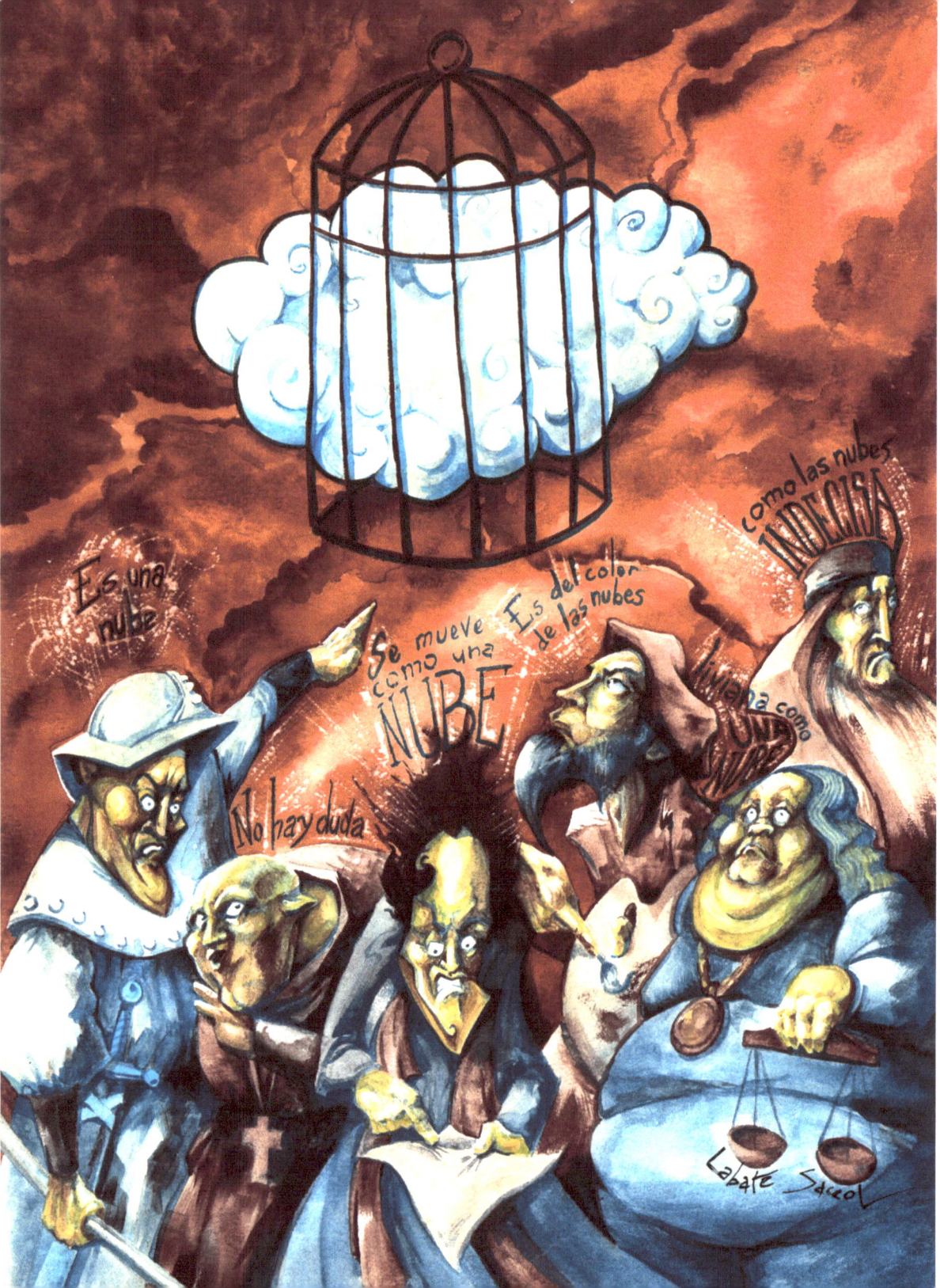

Artist:
Lucía Corral
Spain

URL:
www.menudinha.com

The moon, oh how it shines
How it reflects my breath,
My breath that is slipping-
That of which like my love, And I can't wait,
Can't wait for death to take,
To take my soul, to release me,
To release me from this pain, the pain of life.
The moon, it calls, it calls my name and it says;

„Death is calling, asking...

Do you want to play?"

Written by: Shane, Shiloh

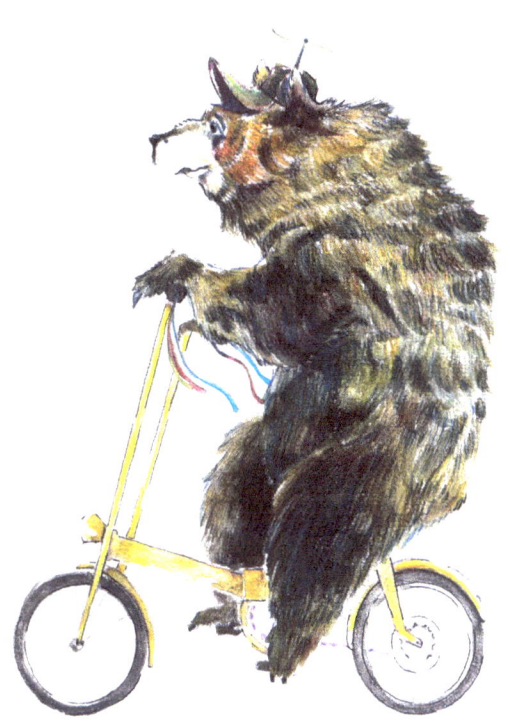

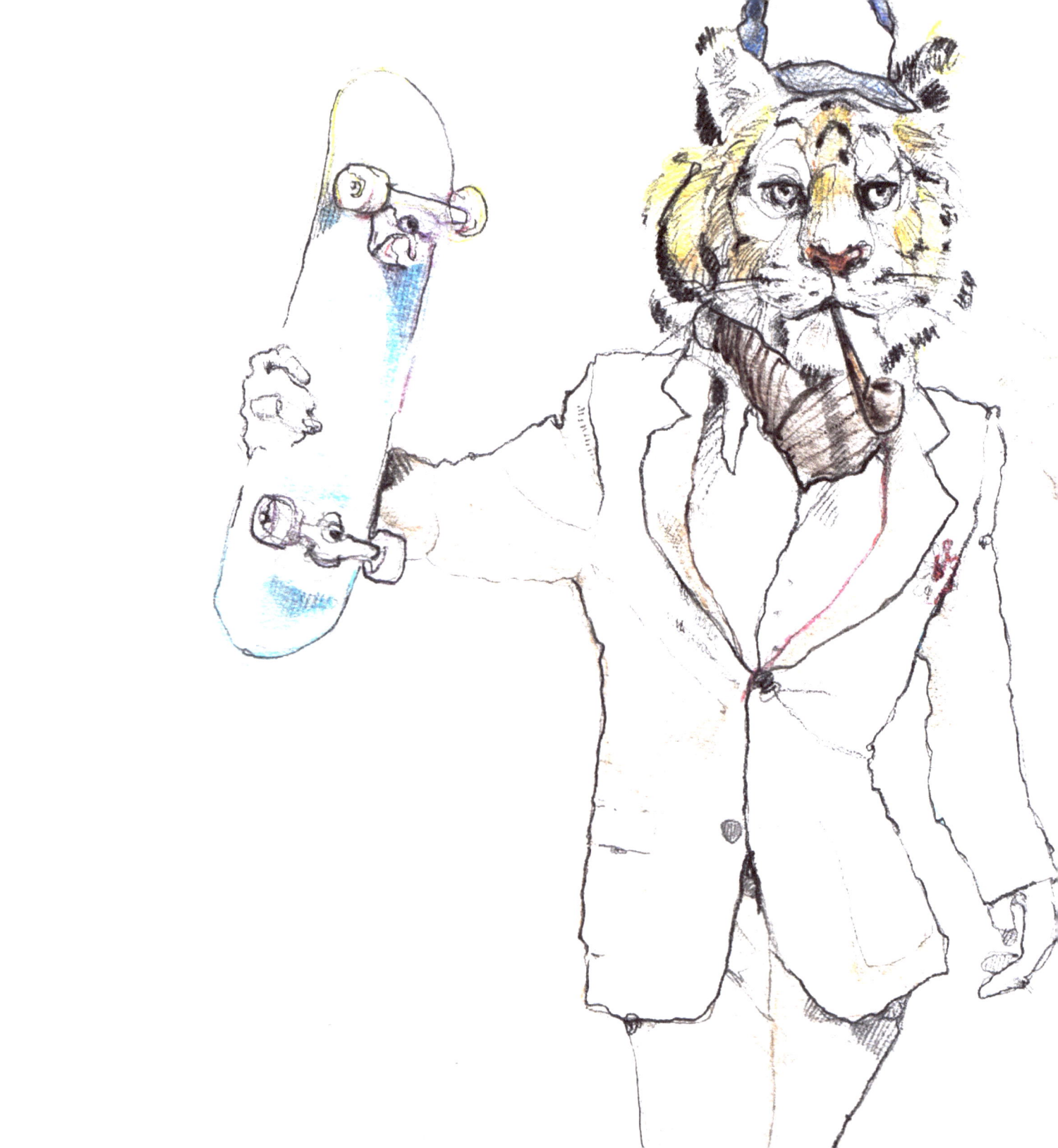

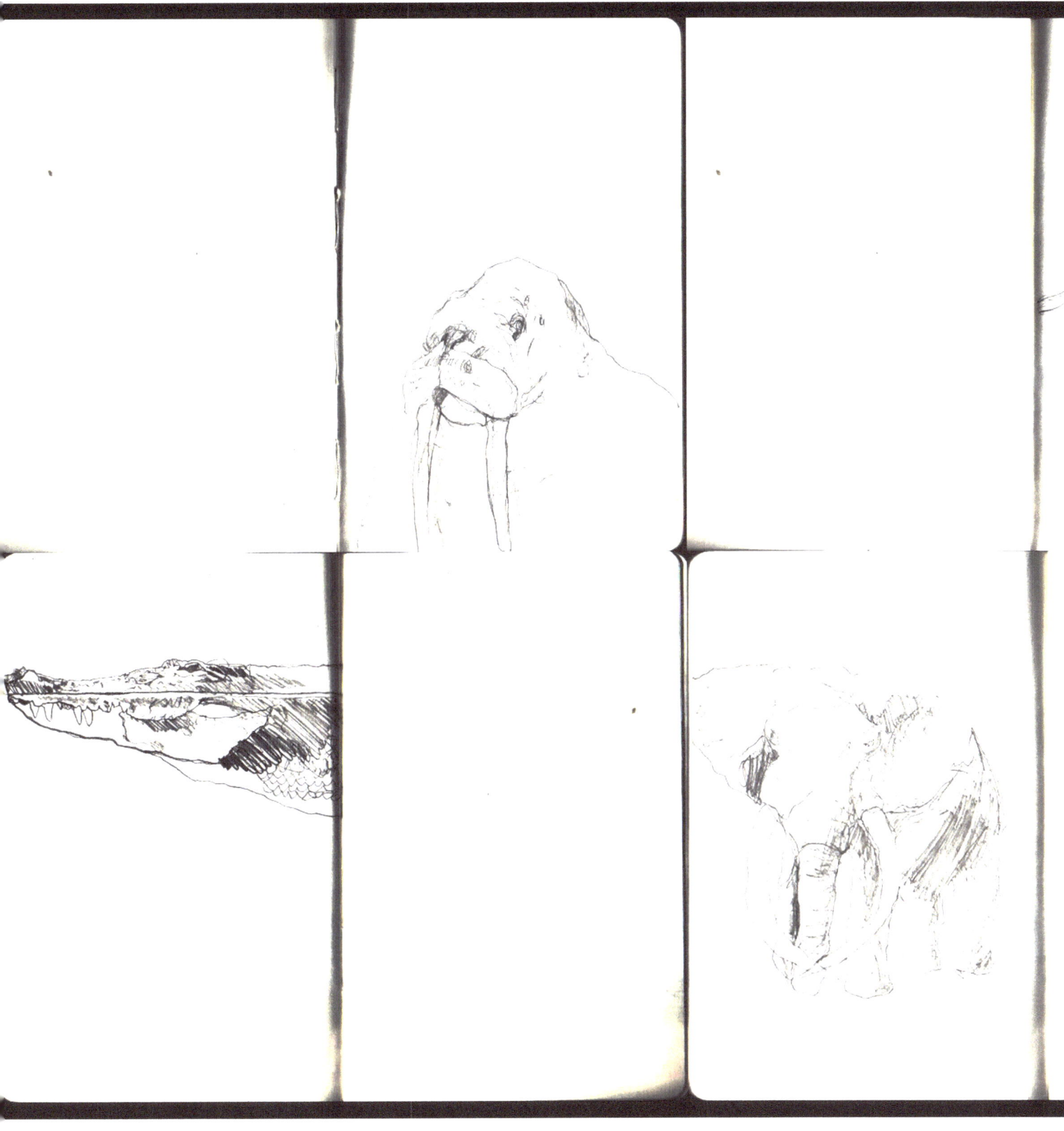

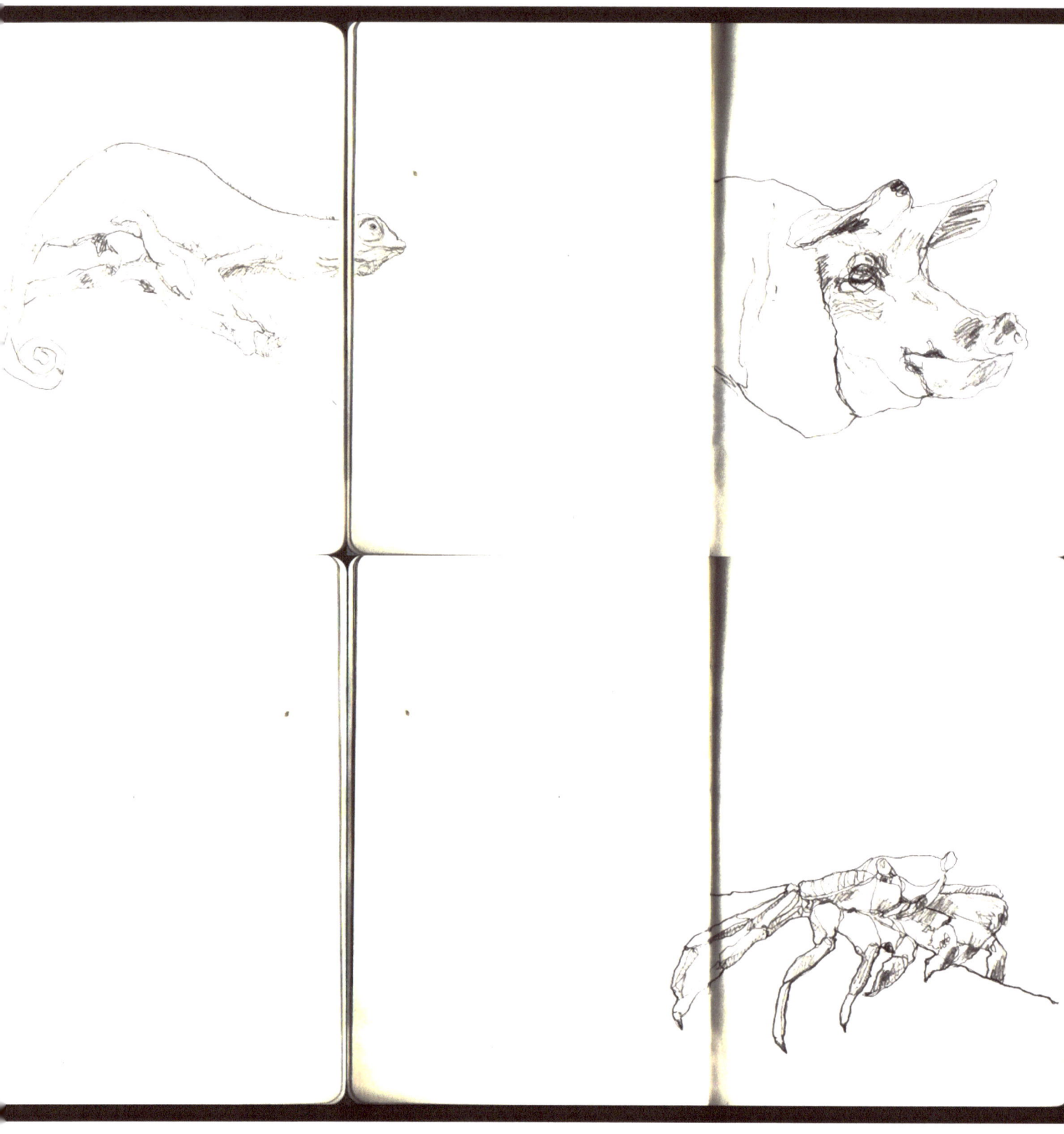

Artist:
M. A. Noreña
Colombia

URL:
www.flickr.com/photos/marsfromvenus/

In the vortex of a fury
you are the greed
in an apple
casting an eye
on the strait of Gibralta
fuelling a sense of angst
without the slightest remorse
configuring which is
making lawmakers reinvent
wars on the placid
hemisphere of civilizations.

Written by: Nikhil Nath

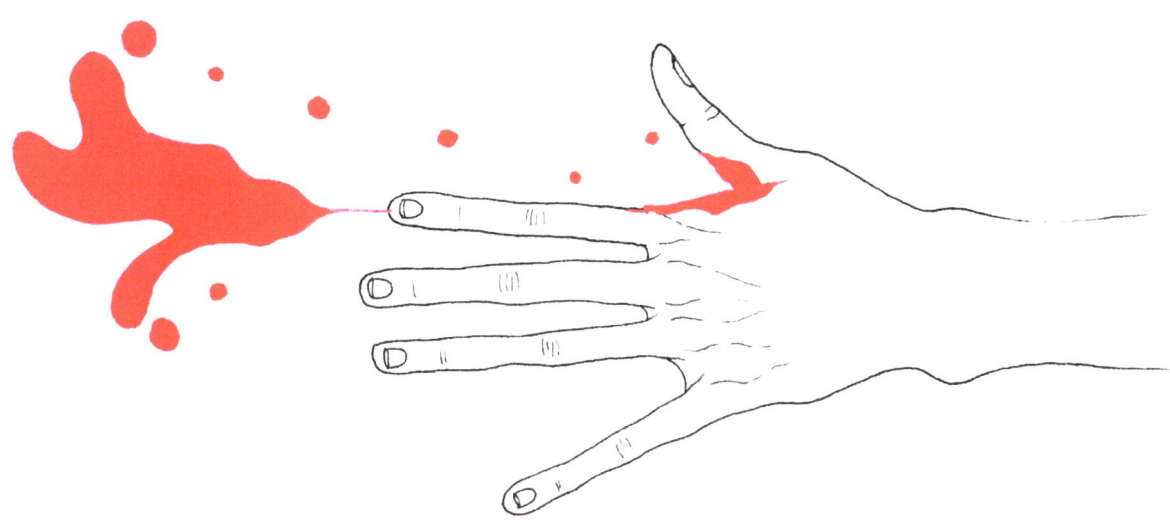

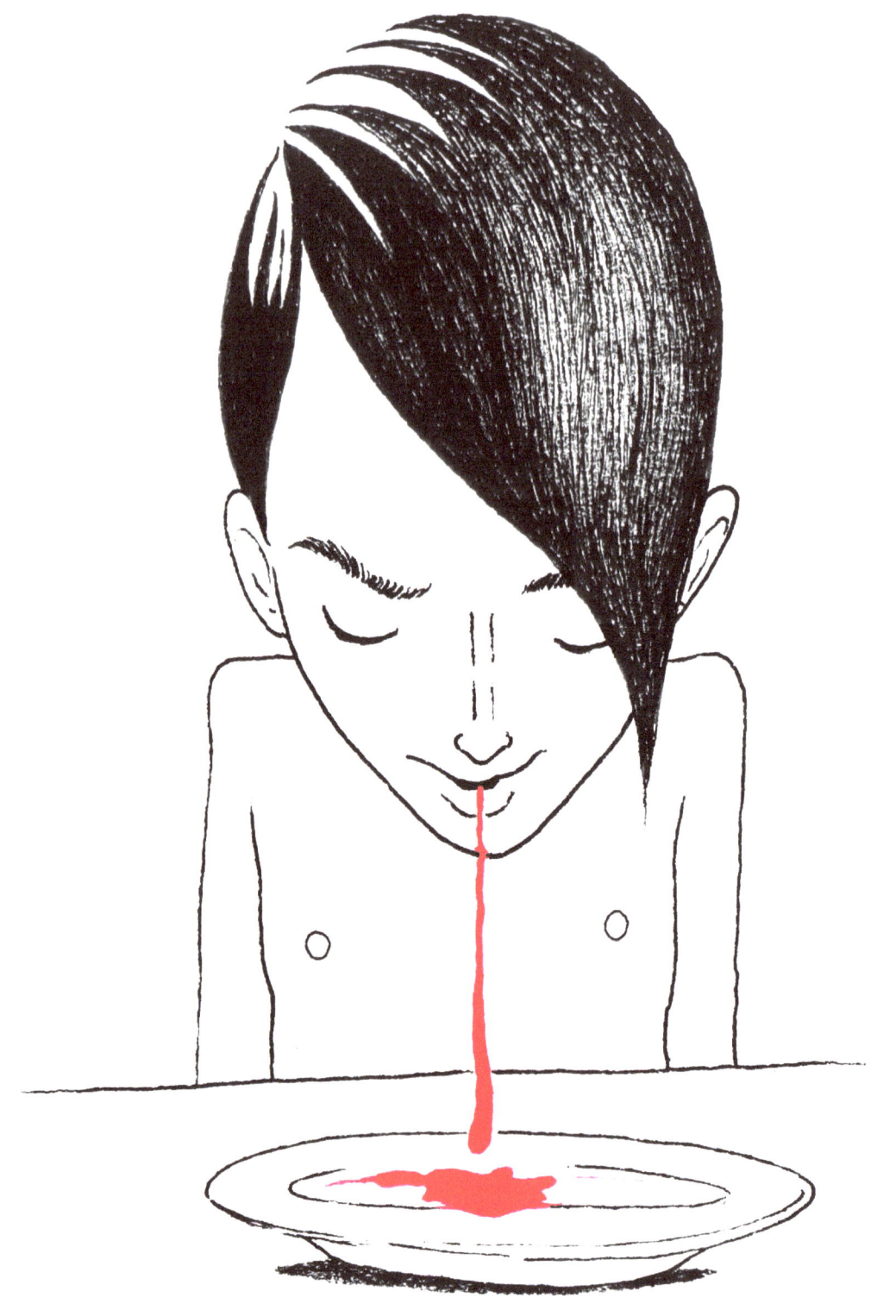

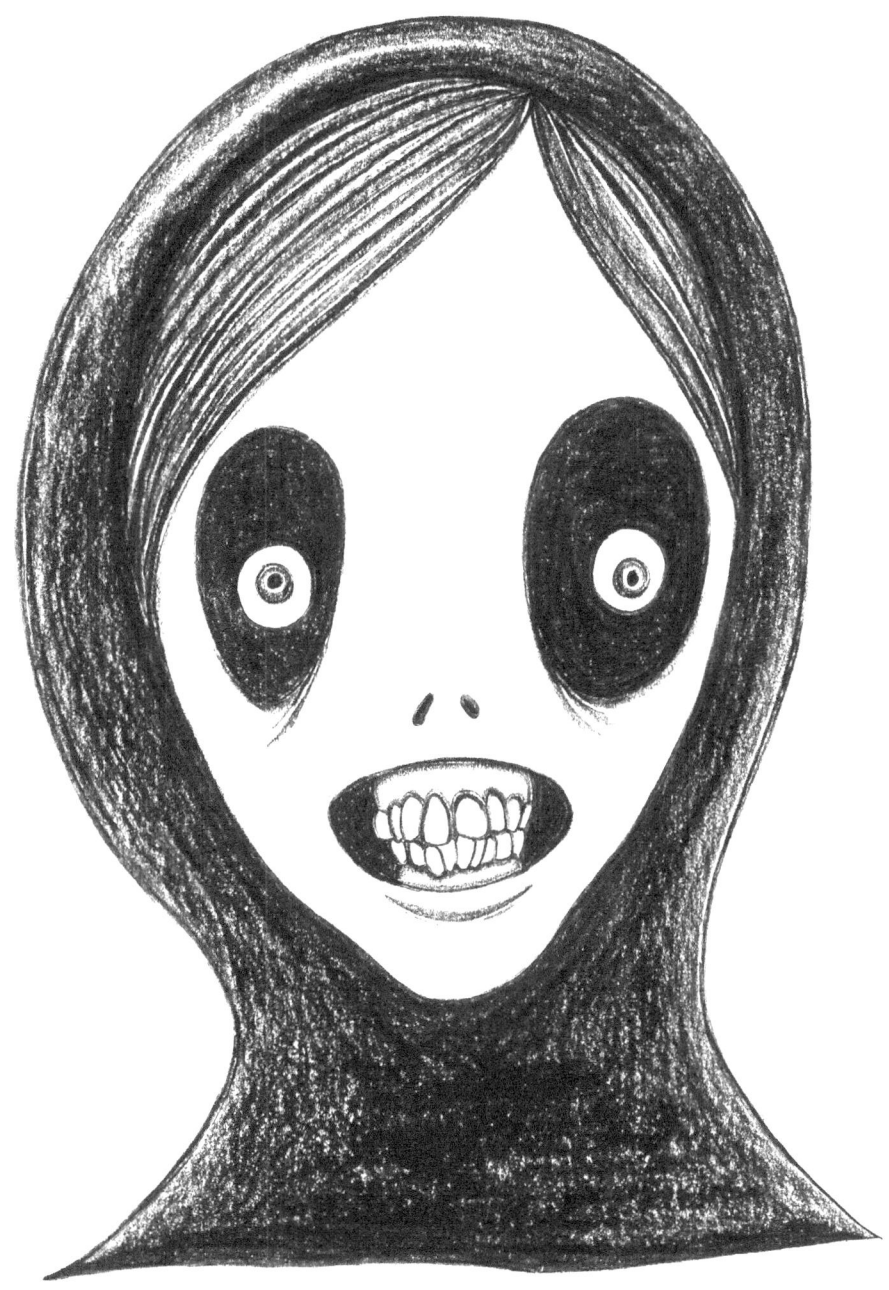

trato Moderno 3, Bú (autorretrato)

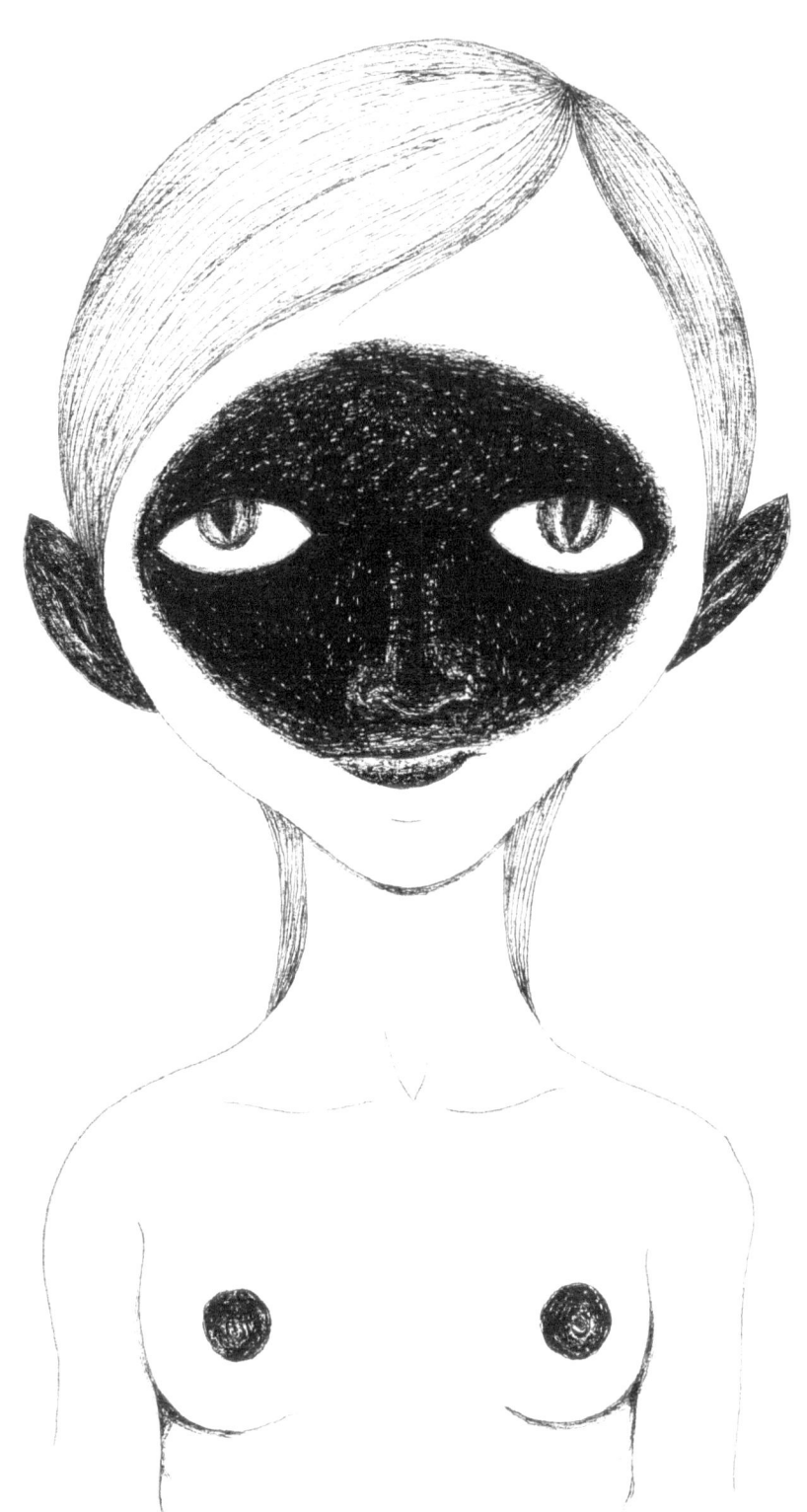

Retrato Moderno 4, Siam

Artist:
J. Jesús Fernández
Spain

URL:
www.jjfez.com

The diamond in my eye
is only a tear drop
entrapping a mountain
in a local train
as coffee wakes up
the bridge of surprise
catching the moon in
a trance across fingers
softly peddling flowers
with the assistance of dreams
melting down my neck
in a swift exchange of letters

Written by: Nikhil Nath

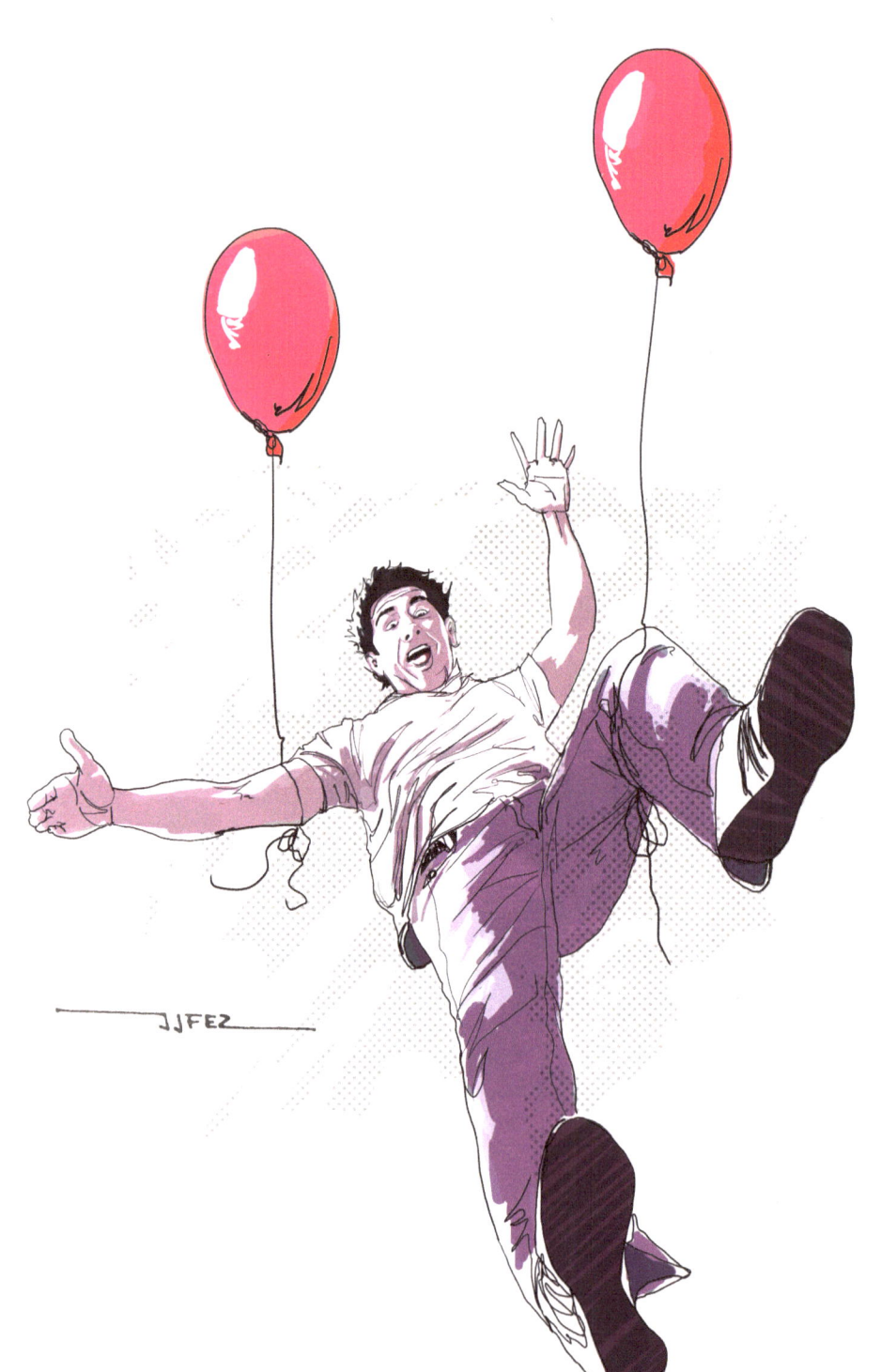

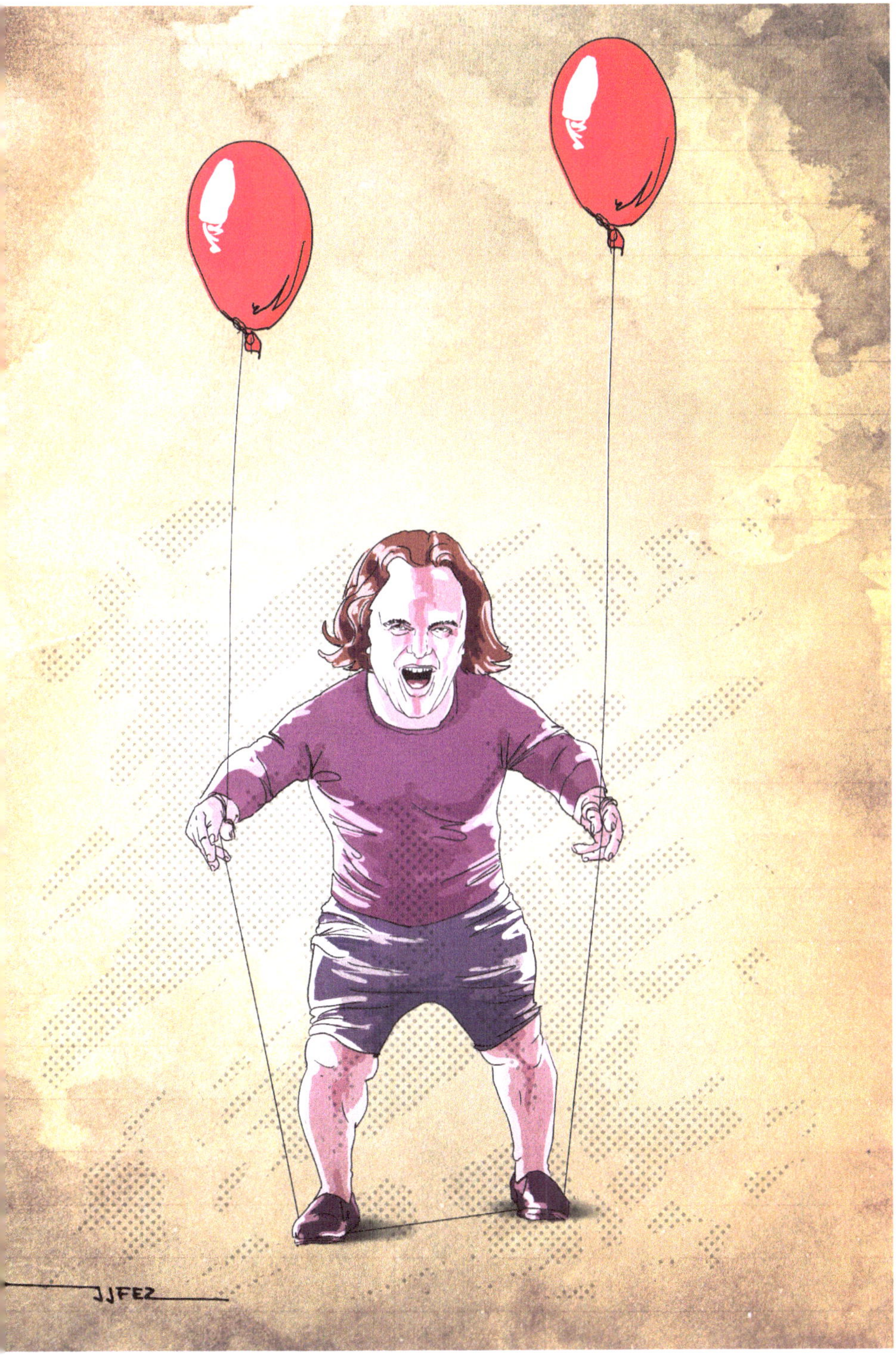

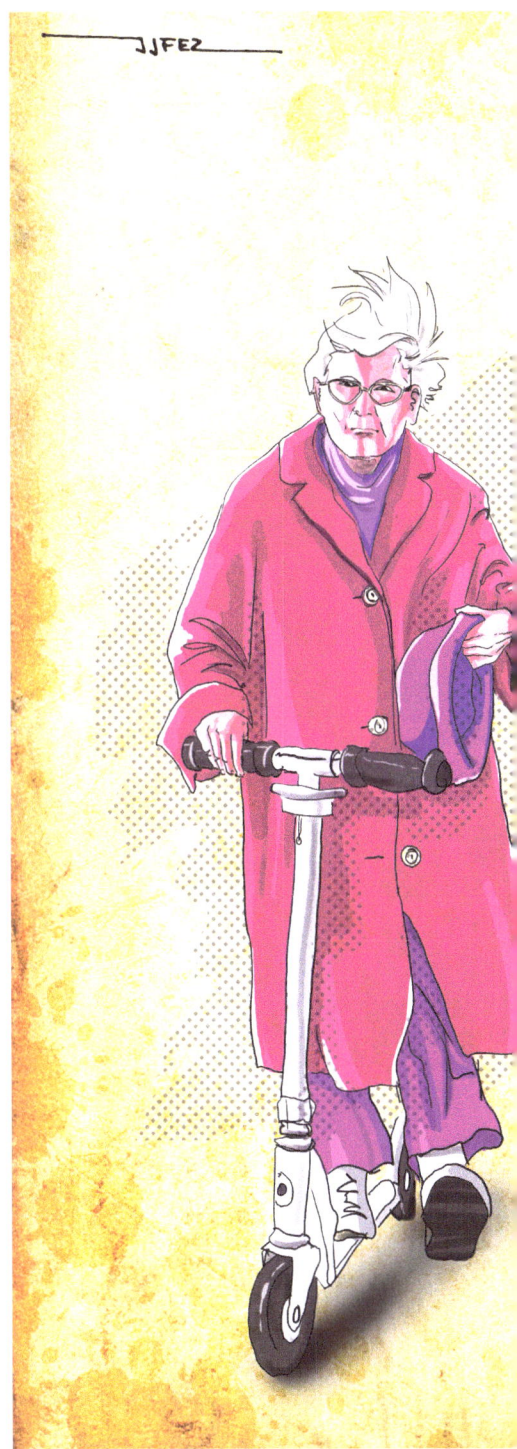

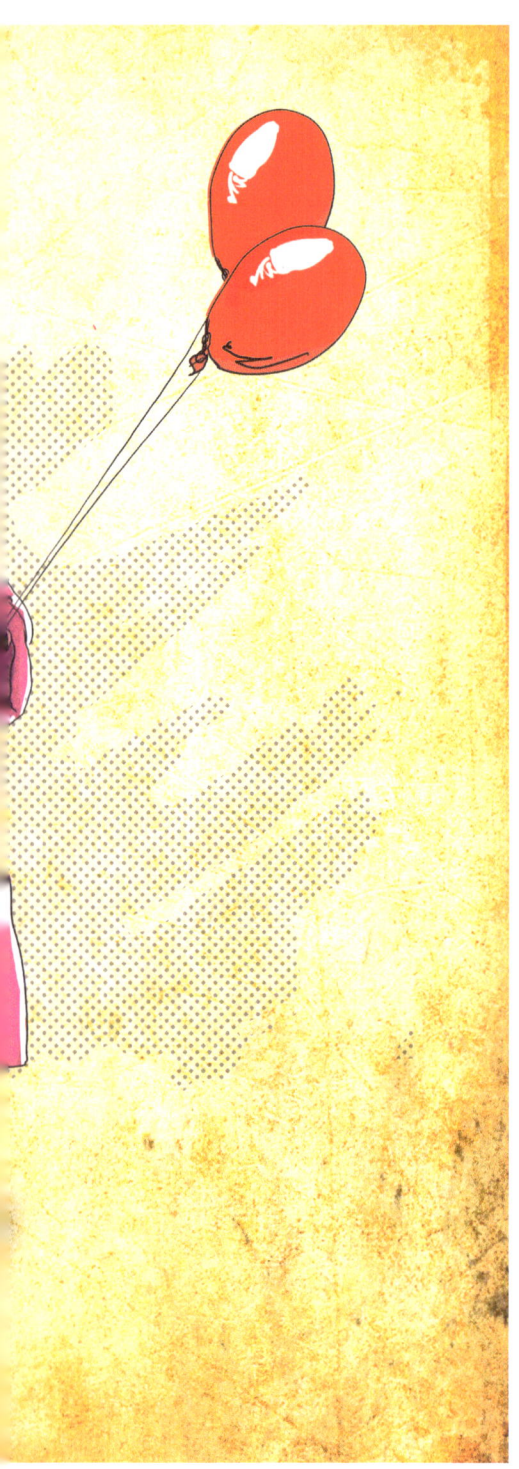

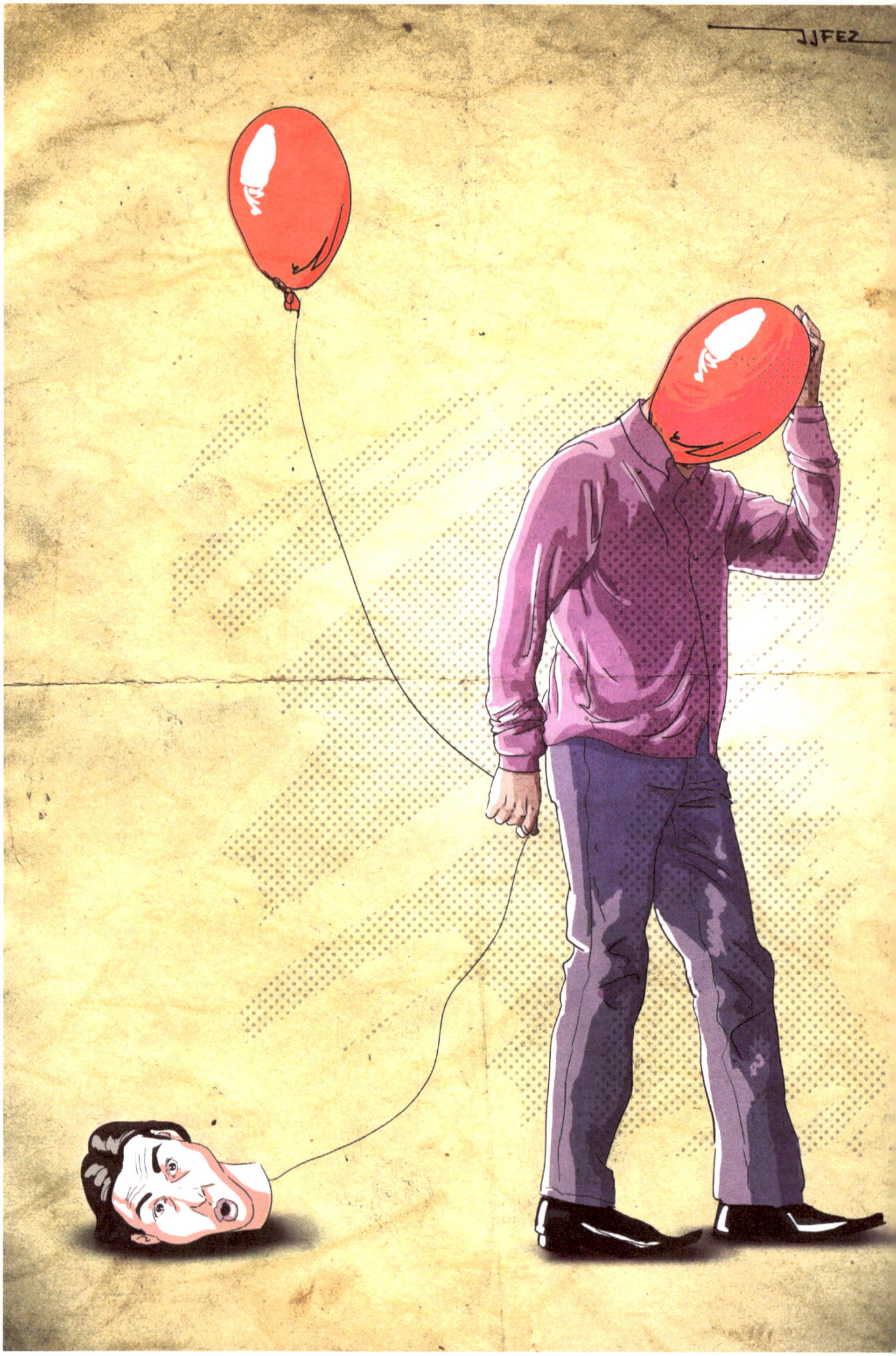

Artist:
Arya Richir
Indonesia

URL:
www.theloop.com.au/aryarichir

once a boy, who's confused.
misled, basically misused.
and he thought „if i do this one, cool"
so he did it and his brain got lost.
while he was loose...
locked in a world.
where he thought he had control.
except he lost „D CONTROL"
no hope, no faith at all.
1 right, 2 many flaws.
so he thought „its time to change it all."
so that's what i did.
because this time i met God.
so that boy was me, but i'm not a child anymore..
I am a Man, who's life is transform.
I am not the same, I've been reborn.
And i am to blame for the mistakes i did before...

Written by: Alex P. Jean Baptiste

Rebirth

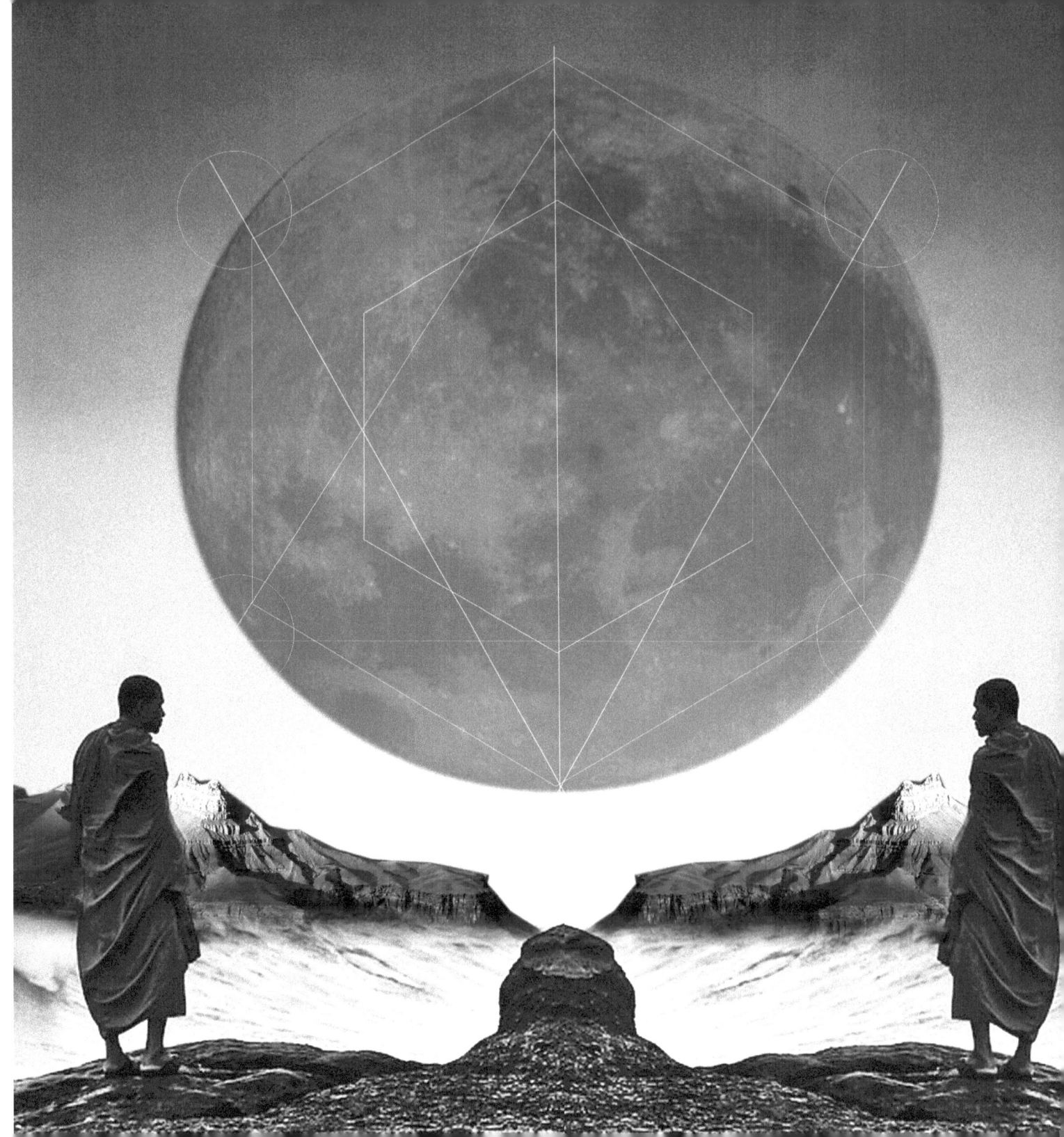

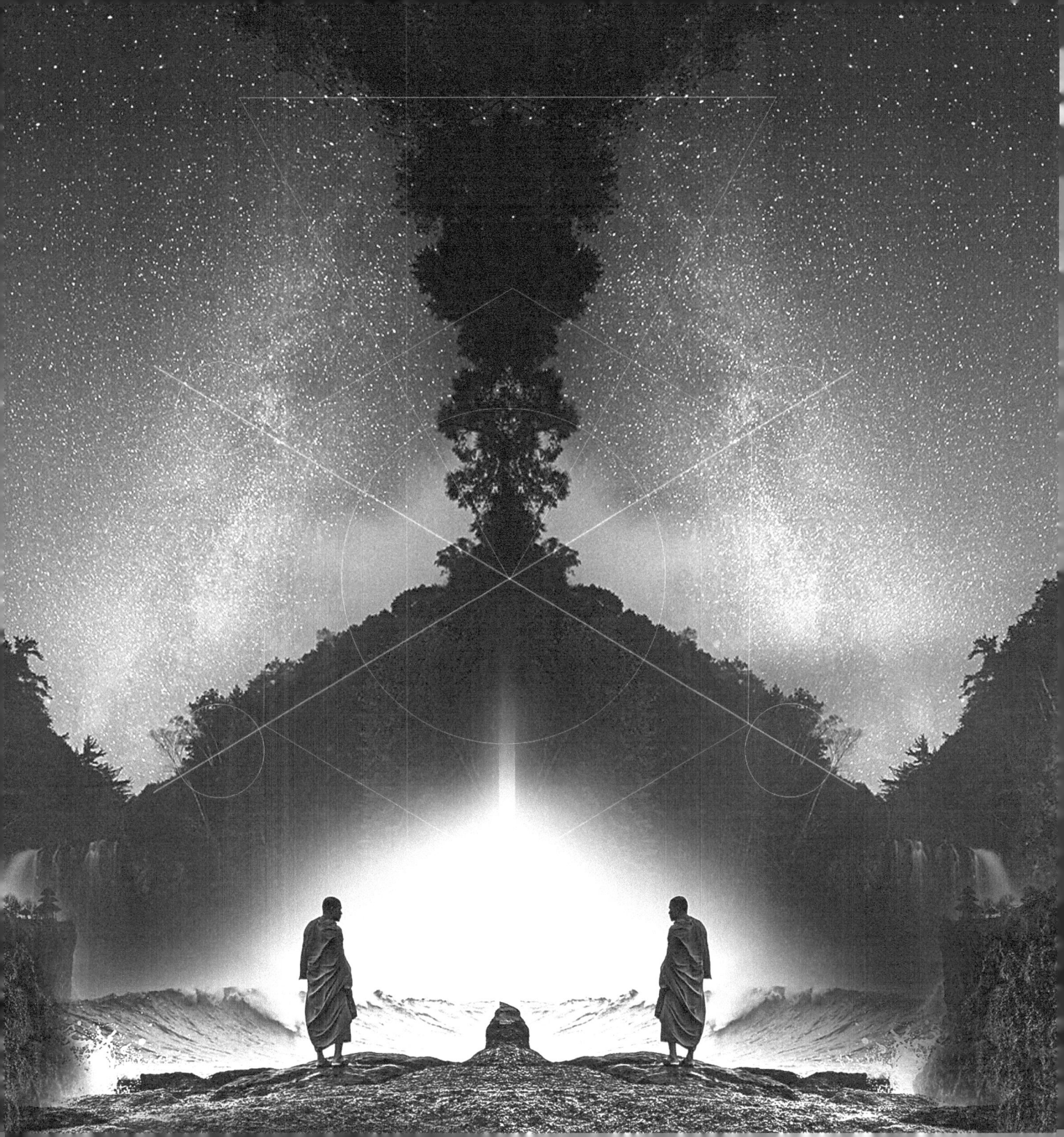

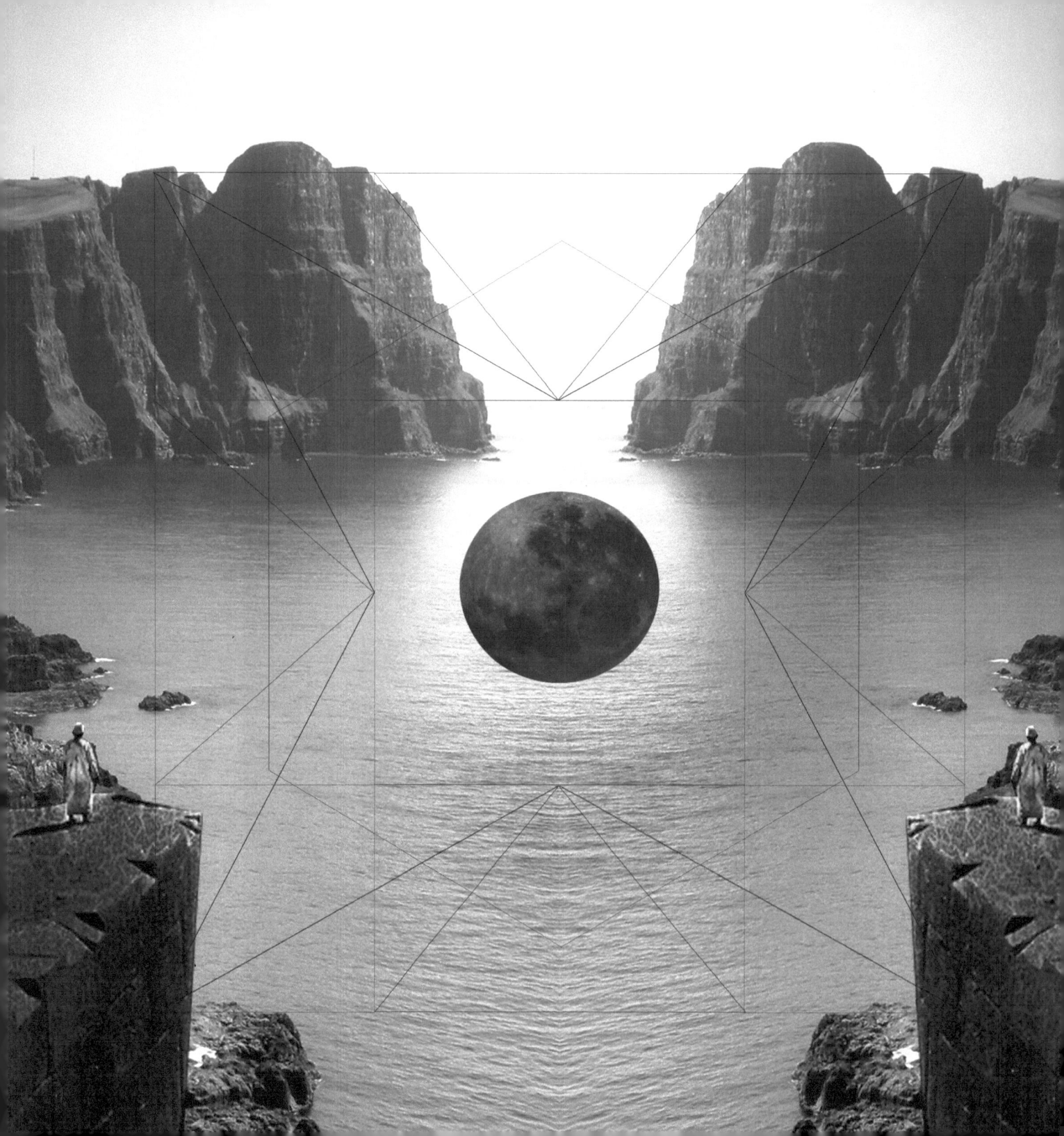

Artist:
Paz López
Spain

URL:
www.pazlopez.com

Let's take off our faces tonight,
Remove the layers of skin,
That make us so uptight.
Stand before me; wear nothing but flesh,
Look wounded, every detail of your inner being exposed,
Let me see right through to your core,
Muscles, veins, organs, all that looks raw.
Remove all that is tainted by this world,
That skin, the cloth of prejudice and pain,
That voice, conformed to complain.
Let me admire your simple being,
Without voice or skin,
For all that is naked,
I see with fair eyes,
A just equality if only for one night.

Written by: Nichola Jade Wong

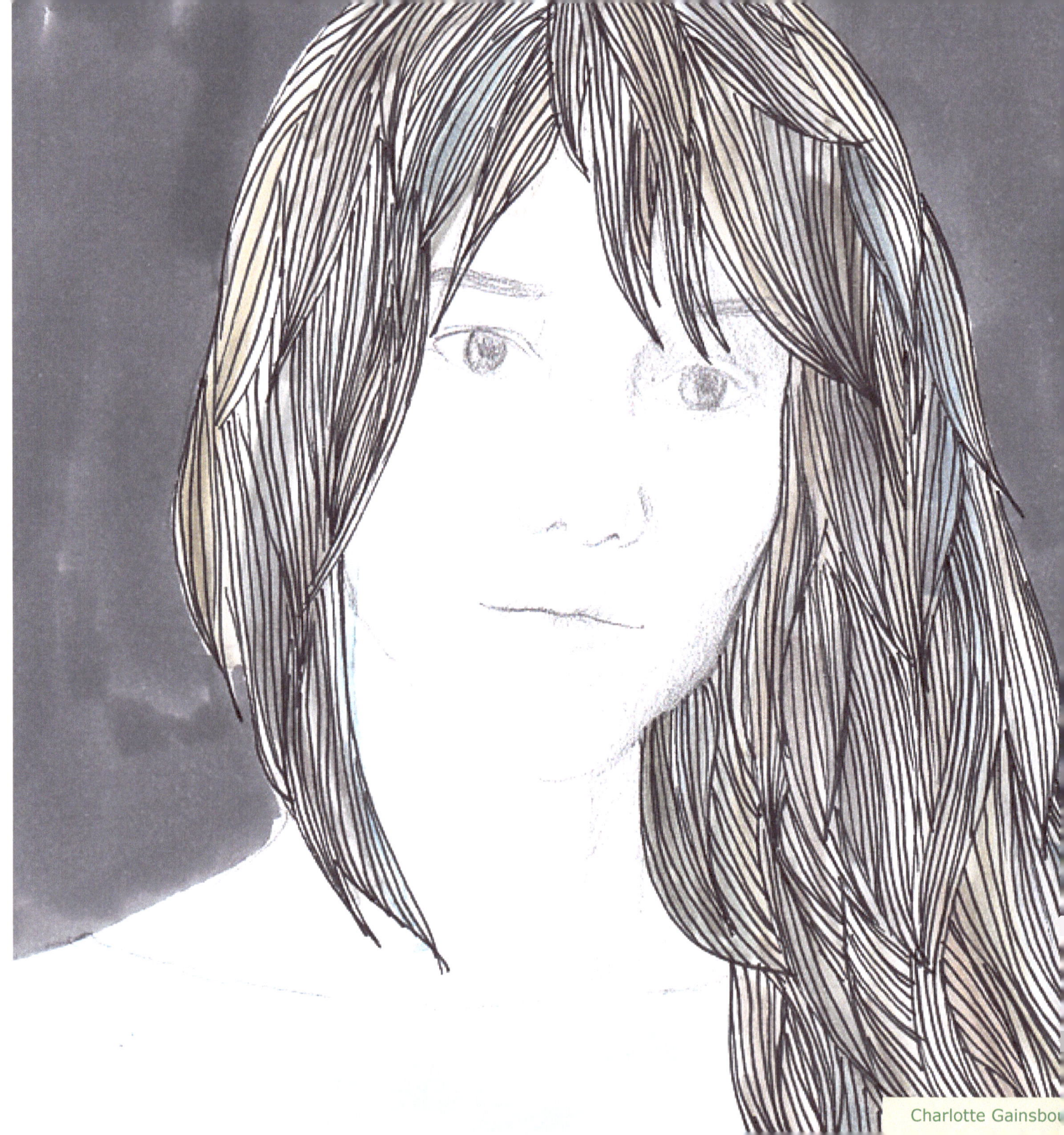

Charlotte Gainsbou

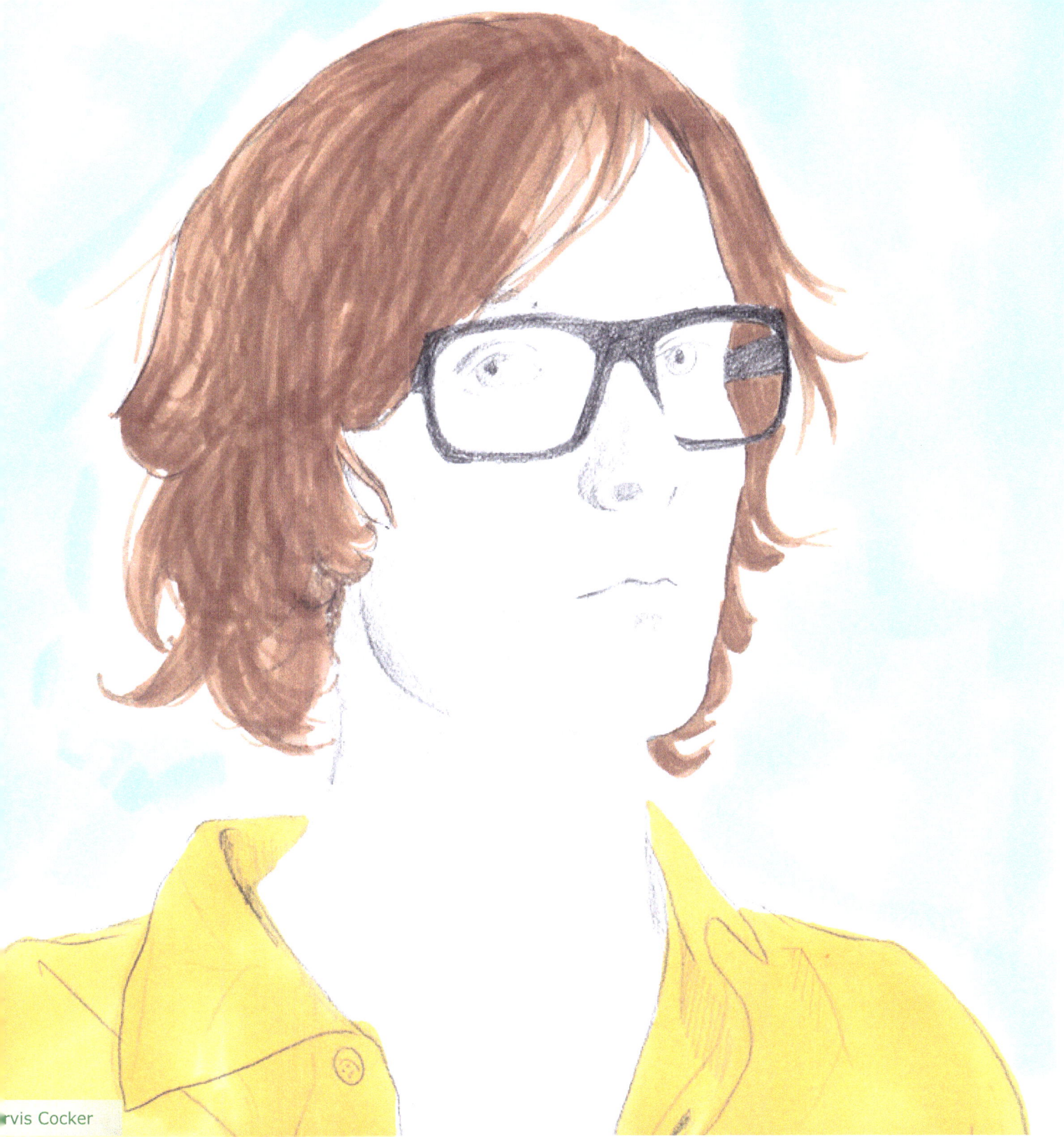

rvis Cocker

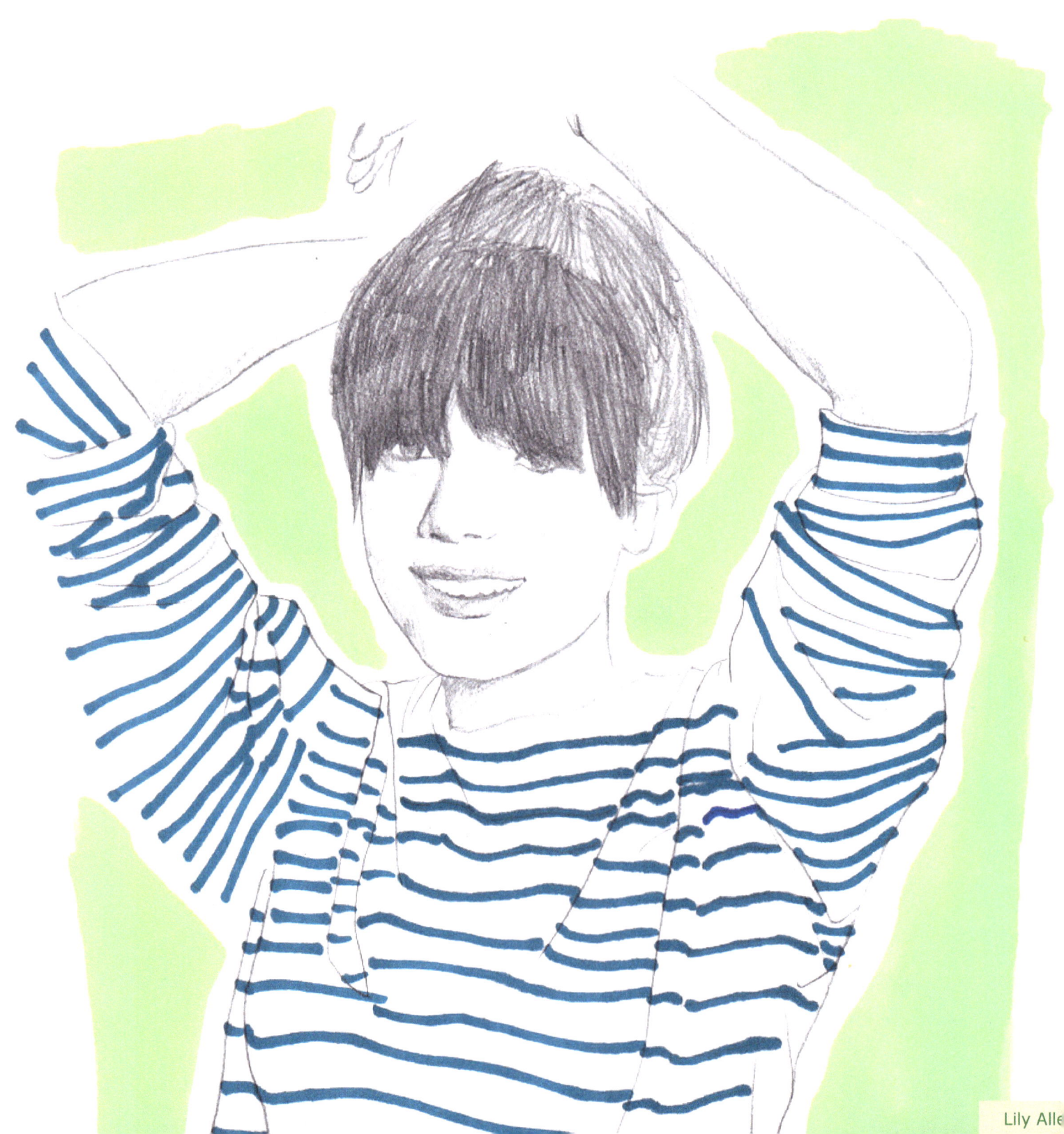

Lily Alle